MW01623233

# Transformation by Design

A Multi-Dimensional Model
of
Inner Healing and Spiritual Formation

by David Takle, M.Div.

# Transformation by Design

A Multi-Dimensional Model of Inner Healing and Transformation

by David Takle
david@KingdomFormation.org



Published by Kingdom Formation Ministries
ISBN: 978-0-9890069-7-2 (soft cover)
ISBN: 978-0-9890069-8-9 (Kindle)

# Transformation by Design

## Table of Contents

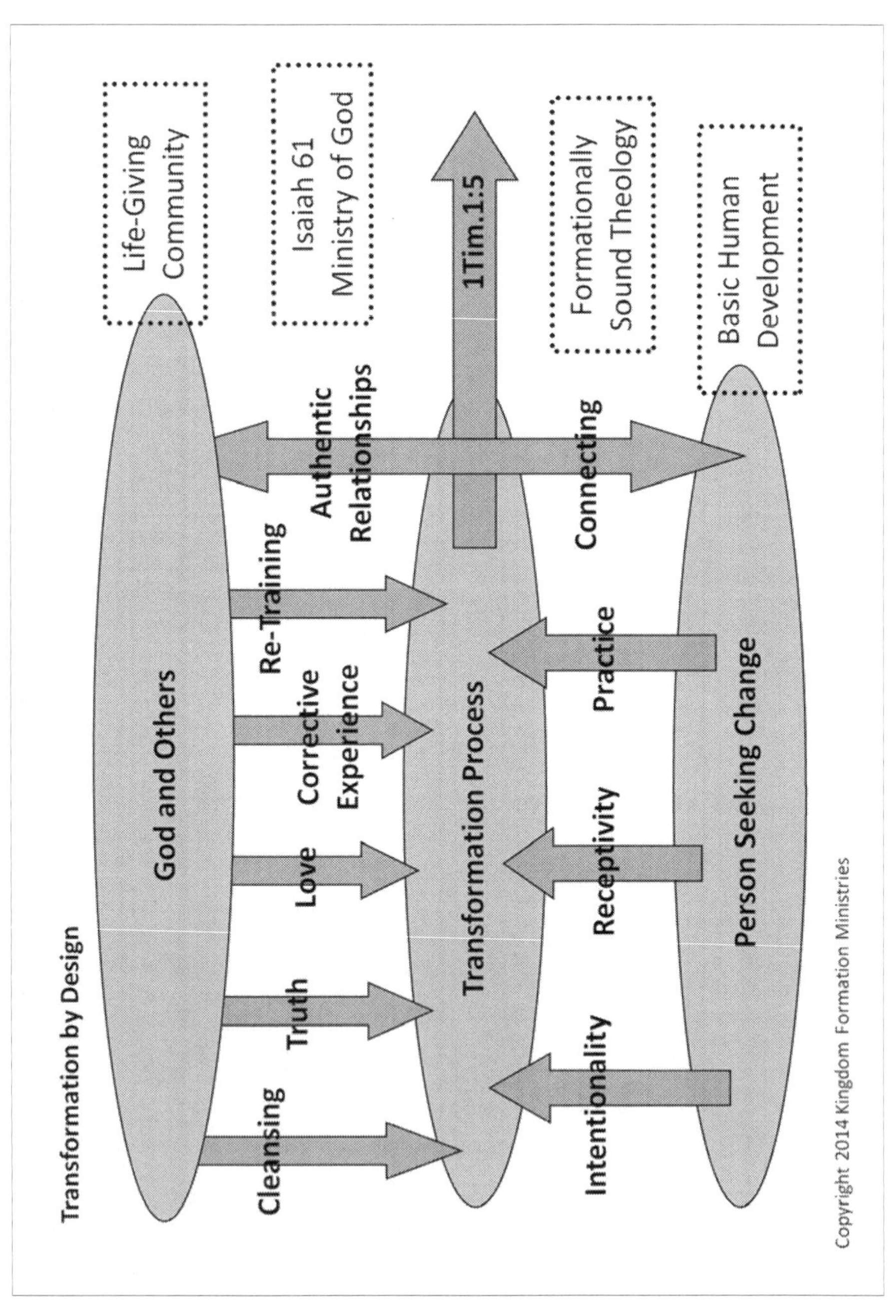
Transformation by Design
God and Others
Transformation Process
Person Seeking Change
Cleansing
Truth
Love
Corrective Experience
Re-Training
Authentic Relationships
Intentionality
Receptivity
Practice
Connecting
1Tim.1:5
Life-Giving Community
Isaiah 61 Ministry of God
Formationally Sound Theology
Basic Human Development
Copyright 2014 Kingdom Formation Ministries

# Preface

For the first thirty-four years of my life, I tried as hard as anyone I know to do all the right things a Christian is supposed to do. I studied the Word, memorized hundreds of verses, taught adult Bible classes, went to Bible college, worked in my local church, attended conferences – the list goes on. But the more I learned, the greater the gap I saw between my own spiritual journey and the kind of victory I saw portrayed in the New Testament. In fact instead of growing spiritually, my personal life declined dramatically over the years in ways that made no sense to me. I was seriously isolated, judgmental of others, harsh with my children, and filled with self-hate. With each passing year, I became more pessimistic, more disillusioned, and more desperate.

Finally in August of 1985 in utter despair I cried out to God. After two days of wrestling and anguish, I arrived at a startling discovery which changed the entire course of my life. As I said it out loud, I could feel the ground begin to shift under me.

"Whatever it is that I am doing … it's not working."

I suppose that should have been obvious, but it was probably the most intelligent thing I had ever said. From that point forward, I became far more teachable and far more willing to be wrong about almost everything. I finally realized that in spite of my knowledge of theology and the Bible, I knew almost nothing about how to live well, and I was willing to start over in order to learn.

Since that day when God broke through to what was an incredibly depressed, emotionally barren human being, He has brought countless resources and experiences into my life that have altered my character, my spiritual well-being, and my relationships in ways I never could have foreseen. Without hesitation I can say that today I am not the person I was thirty years ago.

Along the way I have tried to pay close attention to what sorts of things made a difference in my recovery and what things did not, including all of the help I received from others, the contexts that fostered or detracted from my progress, and the extent to which I myself was involved in the process. But when I stand back and look at this journey I have been on, I am struck by a most peculiar realization – that the life I have now is not due to some spectacular event or angelic vision or any other climactic experience. *Rather, it is due to hundreds, if not thousands of tiny steps available to almost anyone, regardless of where they begin.* The abundant life is not a far-away dream available only to people like Hudson Taylor or John Wesley. The wonders which God mapped out for us in the New Testament are accessible to the very least among us. The great mystery is not how to find this path that leads to life. What is truly perplexing is why it is not more commonplace among professing Christians.

I mean, let's face it – for a faith that loudly proclaims "God can change your life," much of the Christian world seems to have little evidence to support that claim beyond the fact that we attend church on Sundays and can carry on conversations using words not normally heard outside of Christian circles. Some places have even developed doctrines to explain why transformation is so rare today, as if that was God's intention all along.

The truth is that transformation is far more accessible and far more grand than most of us have been led to believe. Nothing about the nature of the spiritual life or God's involvement in the world – or the New Testament for that matter – implies that as Christians we should expect anything less than an ongoing, soul-altering way of life, day by day and year by year.

God has provided us with far more resources to renew our hearts and minds than we can possibly cover comprehensively in a single book, and these gifts include multiple points of intervention, various forms of inner healing, direct mentoring by the Spirit of God, and the inherent power of life-giving relationships.

Once we get a glimpse of how wonderful and broad and deep His provisions truly are, we will begin to see how mistaken we have been to think we could achieve an ideal Christian standard by trying hard to do all that Jesus said to do. Of course we will also see why our efforts have often produced so little fruit.

Transformation need not be rare, nor unpredictable. We can learn how to foster and expect this kind of change so that we become more and more the person God created us to be.

The last twenty or thirty years have seen a tremendous explosion of new resources to help people discover this kind of life. The work done by these pioneers has been nothing short of amazing. Still in spite of all that is available, only a small percentage of the Christian world today seems to be aware of this wonderful revolution that is underway. Furthermore, since we are still in the process of rediscovering how God changes lives, there are precious few comprehensive works on the subject that are written for the benefit of the average layperson.

My hope for this book is that it will cast a vision for transformation that can be embraced by Christians everywhere. We have within our grasp the tools we need to retrain our people in how to engage with God and others for change – the kind of change we all believe really should be possible for the children of Almighty God. I do not claim to have the final word on this subject. But perhaps this model will become a focal point for more analysis and practice, leading to an even more robust understanding of how God changes lives.

# Chapter 1
## An Invitation to Transformation

We have all heard stories of people whose lives were transformed. There is the proverbial town drunk who is now leading a non-profit organization for recovering addicts; the former rock singer who wants to be a missionary; and in Victor Hugo's *Les Miserbles* there is the ex-convict Jean Valjean whose amazing character transformation has captured the imagination of many generations. These are wonderful examples of what is possible, and we hold them up as hope of what God can do to change lives.

Unfortunately, these stories sometimes present transformation in ways that are almost too good to be true, using images that are so dramatic we may have difficulty relating to them at all. Not only are these visions hard to connect with, they also seem to be incredibly rare, larger than life, or once-in-a-lifetime kinds of events. The possibility of transformation as a way of life does not even come up for discussion. What's more, very few of us have ever been mentored by those who could tell stories of ongoing change in their own soul or who could show us how to foster a life filled with growth and change.

Consequently, most of us think of transformation as a rather unusual sort of thing, an entirely unpredictable experience which rewrites a person's entire life script in a single moment. That perception then diminishes our hope for change by any means other than hard work on our part. We hear over and over that if we simply care enough and try hard enough, God will give us the strength to do the right things. And such deeply mistaken words reinforce our belief in personal direct effort as the best means for growing up spiritually. All this despite the fact that the Bible teaches quite clearly that our best effort will bring us to the end of ourselves and is of no value in the fight against sin or the many destructive devices of the enemy.

But what if transformation is precisely what God intends to be our way of life day by day? What if transformation was meant to be commonplace and an ordinary part of Christian experience? What if "being transformed from one degree of glory to another" (2Cor.3:18) is a process God intends for every one of us?

By the time I was nineteen I knew something was terribly wrong, not only in my own personal life, but in the way I had been led to believe that the best we could do was try hard to be good and hang on until Jesus comes back. No one around me really expected to grow very much beyond accumulating more information and making more resolutions. We could go through a new study, memorize a few new verses, take part in a church ministry, or "take a stand" against some new danger that was looming in the surrounding culture. But that was all we knew, so we called that spiritual growth and encouraged each other to keep trying. Most Christians I knew did not even think transformation was much of an issue. After all, we had the Word, we knew what to do in order to be "obedient" and that was all there was to the Christian life. Transformation was only something those really bad sinners needed when they got converted.

It was sometime during my first semester at Bethel College in St. Paul when I came to the realization that if this was all the Christian life consisted of, the New Testament could have been a whole lot shorter! And a lot of what Jesus and Paul had taught would have to be reclassified as unrealistic ideals which had little to do with the everyday existence of normal people. Maybe the apostles and a few super Christians could relate to "the abundant life." But most of us could only dream of such things and had to settle for trying hard to be good and not sin.

However, I could not get past the "what ifs" that kept haunting my mind. What if God meant for us to become more and more like Jesus? Not just learn how to mimic what He said or did, but actually develop a heart of compassion and a sense of wisdom and character that He possessed. What if there really was such a thing as an abundant life? What if we had actually lost our way, and no longer knew how to encounter God in ways that would transform our soul step by step? What if Jesus meant it when He said those to whom He would give His Spirit would have a well of water spring up inside them and pour out from them? What if we could "grow up in all things" as Paul prayed? What if everything they said was all true?

Well here's the good news. *That kind of life really is possible*!

I am not talking about a health and wealth gospel, or an easy life, or a special prayer that will magically change our life. Rather, this is about a way of proceeding that can change our very character, day by day, "becoming more like Him" (1Jn.3:5) through hundreds of incremental changes in how we think, what we value, what we do when things are hard, how we respond when things go well – changing our basic identity and every aspect of who we are in this broken world.

And here is even more good news … I did not make any of this up! The Bible tells us over and over about a life-changing relationship with God. And while many of us have learned how to gloss over high-sounding passages that talk about becoming more like Christ, the truth is that as we learn how to actively pursue the good things God has for us, our life will naturally begin to change in new ways. And this is not hard to do. People all over the world are now in the process of rediscovering how God meant for us to grow and develop as His children.

The bottom line is this: *The kind of life Jesus calls us to is absolutely impossible without transformation*! We can try hard to imitate that life. We can even care a great deal about living well. But unless we are changed inside in ways beyond what we can accomplish by our own resolutions, we will never be able to love, forgive, forbear, overcome temptation, or extend ourselves from a heart of joy like Jesus did.

Perhaps even more to the point, what Jesus actually called us to is a transformative life! God's redemptive purpose is to overcome evil with good[1] and to restore what has been lost. That includes us. As we are changed, God's Kingdom is fleshed out in our body and our three dimensional world. We then become first-hand witnesses to what God is doing on the planet and in human lives. Our gospel moves beyond how to go to heaven when we die and becomes an invitation to another way of life – one that brings about healing of old wounds, power to overcome sin, and an infilling of love and grace that pours out to others. God has called us to be changed, to foster change, and to lead others to change. That is the Great Commission (Mt.28) and what it means to be a disciple and to disciple others.

Often these movements toward Christ-likeness can look like relatively small developments in our spiritual growth. But when changes like this become a common-place experience, our incremental growth compounds over time and transforms us more and more into the image of Jesus. For example, I was struggling for a while over the issue of what it means to be in the will of God. My basic dilemma was, "How can I ever be in God's will when my inner life is such a mess?" As I wondered about this and listened for God's response, it came to me in a rather surprising moment of clarity that God's will is *restoration*, not instant perfection. Which meant that by actively pursuing God's process of restoration, I was living in the very center of His will. What a relief that was! What wonderful confidence it gave me in my relationship with Him!

While this might seem like a simple insight, in that moment it was exactly what I needed from Him, and it felt like walking into another room that was full of light and promise. And this breakthrough became the basis for a new way of relating to God that helped me to be more transparent before Him, with far less self-condemnation.

1 Overcoming evil with good is *The Divine Conspiracy* (Dallas Willard)

When we read the New Testament through the lens of how God actually intends to transform us, it begins to hold together and make sense in ways we never saw before. Anything less requires us to water down the Word or relegate our faith to a set of abstract ideas that have little to do with our day to day existence.

Transformation is real and readily available to all who will learn how to engage with God for change. We need to renew our vision and see that this is truly what God intends for us, and then we need to relearn how to work with Him for the work He desires to do in us. My hope for this book is to paint a picture of how wide and high and deep transformation really is, and to show how we can all work together to create a spiritual climate that supports this process for all who desire to become more like Jesus.

## Defining Transformation

Before we go any further, it is important to be clear about what we mean by the word "transformation." For our purposes here, the working definition we are going to use will be as follows: *Transformation is a genuine change in some aspect of our character such that we become more Christ-like in nature.*

Please note that each phrase in this definition is important. First, as will become more evident later, the changes we are talking about have to do with *character* not simply behavior. We are all quite capable of doing something we do not really want to do, or not doing something we feel the urge to do. Parents often insist that siblings say "I am sorry" to one another when in fact neither one is truly sorry for what they did. Every day people restrain themselves from retaliating over some injustice when they would actually prefer revenge. And most people routinely keep themselves from acting on lust, envy, and other base urges that run through their body. But outward behavior is not what constitutes Christ-likeness. Jesus is interested in changing our heart so good things come out of us by nature, whereas external compliance is what He called "cleaning the outside of the cup."

Transformation is about changing our very character, because that is what produces lasting change in behavior. Good fruit comes quite naturally from a good tree. If we can engage with God in ways that allow Him to remove hate and revenge from our heart and to give us understanding and compassion toward someone who hurt us, then we will not have to restrain ourselves from hurting them or from ruminating on how horrible they are, because we will already want what is good for them. Change comes from the inside out.

Second, transformation is about changing *some aspect* of our character, not the whole of it. Transformation is incremental, step by step, as we move toward Christ-likeness. While these changes can at times be quite far reaching in their effects or even change several aspects of character in a single big leap forward, the norm in Christian growth is one step at a time. On a given day, God might heal an old wound that is causing me to over-react to criticism from others. Then a few weeks later He may extend that healing to greatly reduce the criticism I pour on myself for the things I do wrong. Even later He may change my heart so I stop criticizing others all the time. Each step along the way alters some particular part of who I am and transforms my heart and life a bit more.

Third, we are speaking of *genuine* change and not merely appearances of change or resolutions that wear off after a few months. Nor is this merely a way of suppressing awareness of old patterns that have inhabited our mind and body. For example, for many years I almost never got angry at anyone for any reason. I thought getting angry was unnecessary and unproductive, and I simply did not experience the emotion. But as I began my healing and recovery, I was surprised to uncover a virtual mountain of rage about some of the things people had done to me over the years. What I was discovering was not some new anger fueled by misguided therapy, but very old rage that I had repressed so well I had been unable to feel it at all. My way of never getting angry was not some wonderful Christian character trait I possessed, but a strong vow I had made in my childhood to never act or feel anger like I had seen in others. Genuine change only came after I began to uncover my rage and allow God to speak into those areas where I had been injured. Transformation goes far deeper than mere outward expressions of behavior that look more spiritual or biblical.

Moving on, our criteria of authentic change is further encapsulated by the goal of becoming more like Jesus, who *did* good because He *was* good. The promise we have from God is that we, too, can become good on the inside, so that good comes out of us *because* of who we are and not as a result of *repressing* part of who we are.

Christians are not trapped in bondage to sin, such that we are never able to overcome its influence or destroy its roots. I realize this may run contrary to what many have been taught about the "old nature" or about sin in the life of a believer. And later on we will address some of these faulty ways of viewing the Christian life. But when Jesus says that "those who drink of the water I shall give them will never thirst, and out of their innermost being will flow rivers of living water" (Jn.7:38) He was not exaggerating. He was describing an abundant life that is very real and possible for those who learn to drink the water He has to offer. His words do not describe some kind of strong-willed person who is able to repress a fallen nature and encourage a good nature. He is talking about a transformed heart that allows a person to live out of an abundant flow of something God is doing inside them.

Finally, the phrase *becoming more* in our definition is meant to be taken as an ongoing experience, never completed in this life, forever in process, always in movement toward the goal of developing a character that is more and more like Jesus Himself. "Those who have this hope within them are already in the process of becoming more like Him" (1Jn.3 PAR).

## Our Need for Transformation

Lest we minimize our need for ongoing, life-changing transformation, let us take a moment to review where we are coming from and where God wants to take us in this life.

It might be helpful to visualize an iceberg where only about one tenth of the ice is visible above the surface of the water and nine tenths of the ice is hidden below. That is a fairly good picture of how much is really going on inside our mind that we are actually aware of as we interact with people and respond to the challenges of life on a daily basis. Even when we think we have thoroughly analyzed a problem from every angle and tested our feelings against the various possibilities, many of the factors involved in how we reach our conclusions and make decisions are hidden from our view.

For example, when my first son was born I gave a lot of consideration to how I would raise my children. It seemed to me that my parents had done a few things well and a lot of things poorly, and I was not about to make the same kinds of mistakes they had made. Furthermore, I was quite certain that my analysis was right on the mark, because my parents had taken very different approaches to each of the five children, with a wide range of results. So I worked it all out in my head, and one of the conclusions I came to was that I would never tolerate even the slightest hint of "willful defiance" from my sons. That seemed to me to be a non-negotiable point. I even found support for my ideas in the writings of a well-known Christian psychologist at the time.

However, aside from the fact that I knew almost nothing about the differences between true belligerence and the normal developmental efforts of children, there were at least two problems with my assumptions. First, I was primarily reacting to my own childhood experiences of living with a sibling who had absolutely no restraints applied at all. It was actually my fear of living with another four-year-old tyrant which caused me to take a very authoritarian approach to parenting, to the detriment of my sons and their natural developmental process.

Second, I had virtually no exposure to creative parenting styles that have proven to be quite effective across a broad spectrum of child temperaments. Thus, I relied very heavily on methods that were far more punitive than the situations really called for. My sons were truly very good children by nature. But you would never gather that from observing the harshness of my methods and my attitudes toward parenting them.

The point here is that even though I was sure I had worked this all out as rationally as possible, nine tenths of what was really going on in my head had to do with my own painful childhood experiences and the subsequent faulty conclusions I reached in trying to make sense of my family of origin. Without realizing it, my emotions and history were driving my thought processes and creating the context from which I was trying to reason out how to parent better. Consequently, my theories about child raising were mostly an attempt to compensate for my own unhealed past. Had I worked through my pain before trying to raise children, I would have approached it from an entirely different perspective and arrived at a far more loving style of parenting.

The choices we make are not nearly as rational and well thought out as we would like to believe. Rather, we are largely driven by the ways in which we have been formed over time – or more accurately, *malformed* over time. Life in this broken world takes a toll on us in ways we are scarcely aware of. Without direct insight from the Holy Spirit, we almost always interpret our experiences poorly, and then proceed to live as if we had a full grasp of what life is about. Given that our process of trying to make sense of life is itself severely distorted by our own malformation, we are truly lost before we even begin. It is like trying to use a map of Columbus to get around in Cleveland, all the while convinced that despite our frustration, our map is more reliable than the evidence around us which is telling us something is terribly wrong with our navigation system.

This is why we need to be transformed. The life we see portrayed in the New Testament simply will not make sense if we attempt to live out of our best efforts. Paul says, "Do not be conformed to the patterns you learned from the world, but be transformed by changing your entire understanding of life" (Rom.12:2 PAR). Or as Jesus put it, you have to become a good tree in order to produce good fruit.

We cannot become more like Jesus unless we are first changed from the inside. Without transformation we will never be able to love those who hate us, be kind to those who betray us, be patient with those who plot against us, forgive those who injure us, and so on. Jesus asks us to live in ways that are far beyond our natural ability. Unless something happens inside us to change our character, we will never be able to live the way Jesus wants us to.

## Why Don't We See More Change?

If transformation is so foundational to the Christian life, then why do we see so little of it in ourselves and in those around us? Why is it that so many of us experience a growth spurt immediately following conversion, but after that everything seems to slow down to a crawl? Why do we still have the same triggers we had ten years ago? Why do our bad memories cause us so much pain every time they come to mind? Why do we still hate people who hurt us so many years ago?

While there may be a great many explanations for why people find inner change to be a relatively infrequent experience, there are four reasons in particular that stand out as probably the most common barriers to the kind of transformation we are talking about here. And although there is some overlap between these areas, they are worth exploring individually.

## Not Understanding Our Own Inner World

As indicated in the preface, it was not until I was thirty-four that I first began to discover how to foster the process of change in my own life. In working with a variety of support groups and therapists, it gradually became clear to me that there were a lot of things running around in my head which I had never really identified or questioned as to whether they were helpful or not. Like most other people, my ideas about who I might be and how I fit into the world were formed over time through thousands of interactions with other people, some good and some not so good. I generally accepted that I had become the person I was mostly by countless accidents of birth and circumstances. But it had never really occurred to me that this process could be deliberately steered in a desirable manner, or that my inner world could be shaped by any intentional means.

From all appearances, most people seem to be in a similar state of mind. I often meet people in their forties or fifties who are discovering for the first time that their inner life can be different than it currently is. Many of them describe it like waking up from a deep sleep or having blinders removed that they had not even known were there. And often these discoveries only happen after a life-changing event forces them to re-examine their life or moves them to join a small community where others can hear and understand their struggles.

The good news is that we do not have to experience some traumatic event in order to become more aware of our own process. If we will but become as little children who are willing to relearn what it means to live, and then seek God's love and wisdom as we build an authentic relationship with Him, we will find this all to be more than true. We only need to be shown what that means and how to begin.

### Poor Theologies of Transformation

Unfortunately, and perhaps unbelievably, most of the Christian world has actually given up on any real possibility of ongoing transformation as a way of life. For at least two hundred years now, the predominate approach to spiritual growth and development has been to rely almost entirely on education, motivation, and willpower if you want to become a better person. To paraphrase some of our leading theologians,[2] "God helps those who try hard to do the right things."

Frankly, this abandonment of any real vision for change ought to itself be enough to tell us that something has gone terribly awry in the evangelical world. Approaching the spiritual life with willpower is about as effective as pushing against the steering wheel of a car in order to make it go forward. Yet that is what most of us have been taught and what we have passed on to others. I have to admit that I taught it myself for many years. "If we just care enough about what is important, we will make the right choices and do the right things." Except that for some strange reason my heart would often fail to go where I thought it should go.

Poor theologies of sanctification will inevitably block our path to the kind of life we see in the New Testament, a life that is only possible as we change who we are on the inside.

### Lack of Vision

The real tragedy in all of this self-effort is that we lose sight of how God changes lives, and with that, any hope of transformation. The more we rely on our own resolve to do what is right, the less we will ever know of the power of God's truth, of the depth of His love, or of what it means for Him to write His laws on our heart.

Much of the Christian world today is dying for lack of vision. Some are simply unwilling to face the truth about our general anemia; some choose to

---

2 Deiter, et al, *Five Views on Sanctification*

double down on their use of shame and condemnation in an effort to coerce better performance; still others just quietly leave the church when they realize it has very little to offer real people in a broken world.

**Direct Resistance to Transformative Practices**

While the previously stated reasons for the lack of transformation are lamentable, this one borders on the unconscionable. I realize that I am using strong language here, but it is difficult not to.

During the last thirty years or so, we have witnessed one of the most important developments in the Christian world since the Reformation, which is the growth of the spiritual formation movement. For much of this we can be grateful to Dallas Willard, who in many ways blazed a trail and showed us a way of proceeding which had been lost a long time ago. As a result of the work he and others have done, there are now literally thousands of Christians whose lives have been tremendously impacted for good. And the Christian world is far richer for the contributions these wonderful leaders have given us.

However, the resistance to their work has been enormous. And what is most disturbing is the fact that this resistance has not come from the secular world but from certain areas of the Christian world that have taken it upon themselves to condemn any and all efforts to help people enter into an experiential relationship with God. While a thorough critique of their methods is not intended here, suffice it to say that they have in every way possible misrepresented the work of Willard and others, and then attacked these distorted versions of spiritual formation with all the righteous indignation they can muster.

Apparently, according to these heresy hunters, it is alright for us to think logical thoughts about doctrine, but if we actually try to interact with God on a personal basis or expect God to speak to us directly, or if we sit quietly and contemplate the goodness of God long enough to actually feel genuine affection for Him, we are playing around with New Age practices and giving ourselves over to something evil.

If it were not for the damage these critics do in stopping others from discovering what God has for them, their tirades over spiritual formation would be laughable. What they supposedly oppose on the basis of the Bible can be seen on every page of the Psalms and in the lives of all the great saints throughout history. Yet they have managed to nail shut the door to the Kingdom and prevent a great many people from entering (Mt.23:13).

Again, I realize this is rather harsh. But it seems to me that anyone with eyes to see can tell that doctrine and willpower alone do not bring about much change (other than a tendency toward self-righteousness), while on the other hand people's lives are being transformed daily and dramatically by building the kind of relationship with God that comes with well-informed spiritual formation.

Even when Christians are not entirely led astray by such teaching, the impact of these terrible ideas is still felt by large segments of the evangelical world. One pastor of a large church I know of refused to allow his staff to consider a course on spiritual formation because it was based in part on the work of Dallas Willard. He had heard that Willard was "controversial" and did not want to get involved in anything of that sort. What an awful decision! He preferred instead to preach a performance-driven approach to the Christian life that has never had a shred of biblical support.

We need to get past trying to defend things as they are, and instead be willing to be teachable and learn what we missed along the way. If not, we may find ourselves undermining the very things Jesus came to bring us, including an abundant life.

### So Where Do We Go From Here?

The questions we must ask at this point are – How did God intend for us to be transformed? What does it mean to have our minds renewed? What sorts of things contribute most directly to our transformation? How are we involved in the process? And how do we build a context which fosters the kind of life we see embodied in the New Testament? That is where we now turn our attention.

## A Model of Transformation

Throughout the rest of this book we will be referring to the large diagram at the beginning of this book which lays out a functional model of the major elements contributing to transformation. While this diagram may appear rather overwhelming at first, hopefully its basic simplicity will become apparent as we proceed. To help make sense of the diagram it is important to notice that all of the various components are actually divided into just four major areas of concern, and these we will be discussing in great detail.

The first segment of the diagram consists of the upper oval marked "God and Others" along with the five arrows pointing down and the double arrow marked "Authentic Relationships. This upper area captures the six most significant direct causes of transformation. While many other things influence the process of change, in practice it turns out that virtually all transformation is caused by one or more of these direct causes.

The oval at the bottom of the diagram labeled "Person Seeking Change" and the four arrows pointing upward comprise the second major portion of the model, which is about how we are personally involved in the process of transformation. No one is transformed without their own participation. We are always involved in some manner, even though the direct causes come from outside us.

But not just any participation will do, or we would not be having this discussion. For example, nearly all Christians have had the experience of reading large portions of the Bible and being more bored than transformed.

How we are involved in the process matters. And this participation is a learned process, one we need to know about in order to engage well.

The third major segment of the diagram is represented by the four dotted boxes. These boxes represent important contextual elements which help to foster transformation. Supporting contexts not only set the stage for change, they help to make our participation possible and effective. It is very rare, for example, to experience transformation when we embrace theologies that mitigate against it (believe it or not, these are extremely common) or when we are isolated from others who are pursuing a life with God. Context matters. We need as many resources as possible in order to follow after Christ and engage in this process day after day and year after year.

Finally, the fourth aspect of this model is represented by the arrow labeled "1Tim.1:5" ("Love from a pure heart") which is the end goal of a transformed life. This phrase, taken from First Timothy, encapsulates the reason why God wants to transform us in the first place – so we could take on more of the character of Jesus and express His love in our world.

God never meant for His children to merely "hang on 'till Jesus comes." The New Testament authors were very clear about our need to grow up in Christ and to pursue that goal throughout our life. Paul's hope for the church in Ephesus is but one example:

> *Building up the body of Christ, until all of us come to the unity of the faith and of the knowledge of the Son of God, to maturity, to the measure of the full stature of Christ … speaking the truth in love, we must grow up in every way into him who is the head, into Christ, from whom the whole body, joined and knit together by every ligament with which it is equipped, as each part is working properly, promotes the body's growth in building itself up in love (Eph.4:12-16).*

In the last thirty years we have been flooded with an unprecedented level of resources for renewal and growth. Today more than ever we have before us the opportunity to fulfill Paul's vision and change the face of the Christian Church, to say nothing of the glorious impact this can have on each of us individually. My prayer is that we will fully embrace this gift and pursue God for all that He has for us.

# Chapter 2
# Direct Causes of Transformation

What causes transformation? How accessible are these sources of change? How common are they? How do we encounter them?

Referring to the main diagram at the beginning of the book, there are six direct causes or sources of transformation which have been singled out for consideration as the primary movers of change. Significantly, all six of these arise from outside of a person seeking transformation. We do not change our character by our own willpower or by trying hard. Rather, we need God and others to offer us what we do not have. This dependence upon outside help means we become recipients of real grace – receiving from another what we cannot accomplish by our own effort.

In the following sections we will examine each of these six areas in detail to see how they bring about genuine change in character and identity, thereby altering our life. While some overlap does exist between these causes, each one involves some unique aspects in terms of the means by which we engage them and in terms of how they contribute to our overall process of change. Briefly, they are:

***Cleansing*** – Removing the causes and effects of sin and suffering.
***Truth*** – Internalizing how God sees us and our life.
***Love*** – Being known and cared about beyond our wildest dreams.
***Corrective Experience*** – Surprise encounters with new ways of living.
***Retraining*** – Forming new pathways in our mind and body.
***Authentic Relationships*** – Strong bonds with God and healthy people.

Virtually every transformative experience involves one or more of these areas. We will now examine each of these in some detail.

## Cleansing

*Removing the Causes and Effects of Sin and Suffering*

Cleansing is one of the single greatest themes in all of Scripture. One might even characterize the whole of salvation history as a story of how God is in the process of overcoming all traces of evil, purifying and restoring us to be the people He created us to be. Most of the Old Testament laws have to do with describing what sort of things defile people and how they can be made clean again. The New Testament writers pick up that theme in order to demonstrate the limitations of the law, how sin defiles us beyond what can be cleansed by following laws, and how we can be made clean by the work of God.

The author of Hebrews goes to great lengths to explain that while the primary function of atonement under the law was to cleanse people from sin, true cleansing could not come from sheep and goats. It was not until Jesus laid down His life that an authentic cleansing atonement was really possible. Jesus took our sin in His body and then poured out His life, thereby exhausting and destroying the power of sin. He then offers His righteousness to us who believe, so that we may be clean indeed.

Paul also teaches this understanding of the cross, which is sometimes referred to as the "exchanged life."[3] We give up our sin and death to Jesus, and He in turn gives us His life and righteousness. This life then literally regenerates our spirit within us. We are "made alive" in Christ and are resurrected with Christ. Nothing could be more transformative!

But that is only the beginning. We learn from Paul and John and others that this cleansing process continues to transform our natural mind for the

3 "Exchanged Life" is a term coined by Howard Taylor to describe the life-changing realization that occurred in the life of his father, famed missionary to China, J Hudson Taylor

rest of our life, from its old patterns to God's ways (Rom.12:2). Paul says that we can "by means of the Spirit" put to death the things of the flesh (Rom.8:13) and thereby live more fully as God intended. Elsewhere he tells us to continue to "cleanse yourselves from all defilement of flesh and spirit" (2Cor.7:1). John says anyone who hopes for a total restoration in heaven is already in the process of becoming more pure (1Jn.3:3).

Perhaps the most famous prayer for cleansing is found in Psalm 51 where David is overcome with grief because of his moral failure and the things he has done due to his unregulated desires. This is often called a psalm of repentance, which it is. But if we look closely, it bears little resemblance to what most of us have been taught about repentance.

The vast majority of Christians view repentance something like this. First you are convicted of your sin, then you feel remorseful, confess that sin to God, and resolve to not do that any more. God then forgives your sin and you move on and try to do better.

Surprisingly, we see almost none of that in David's Psalm. Nowhere does David promise to never commit adultery again. He never vows to refrain from killing those who fail to help him to cover up his sin. In fact he does not make any resolutions at all. Instead, he comes to God in utter defeat and says, in effect, "God, my heart is far more defective than I ever knew. I need You to create in me a new heart, one that would never imagine such horrible things. Cleanse me of my sin, because I cannot do that myself. Remove whatever is in me that is evil and replace it with your goodness." David did not need to try harder to be good. He needed God to cleanse him of his evil ways. David wanted to be transformed by God, by a thorough cleansing of his heart.

As Paul points out in many places, God is intent not only on removing our guilt and forgiving our sin, but also removing the causes and effects of sin. David knew that as well, which is why he could say with assurance that when God was finished renewing his heart, he would be able to proclaim the wonders of God to sinners and they would come to Him (v.13).

Cleansing removes our actual sin and replaces it with God's righteousness. Our desires change. Our passions and intentions change. We become less hateful, less contemptuous, less harmful, more loving, more compassionate. Those are changes we cannot make on our own. That is why we need to go to God for help (Heb.4:16).

Cleansing can be an experience all its own when we come to God and seek Him for this kind of renewal. However, it often accompanies some of the other forms of transformation as well. For example, when Nathan the prophet pointed his finger at David and said, "You are the man in the story," that parable became for David a *corrective experience* (see below) which then led to his repentance and prayer for cleansing. Such is the process of transformation, where quite often multiple factors merge in a single life event.

Cleansing our sin, our resentments, our unforgiveness, our bitterness – the list is long – cleansing frees us from our bondage and gives us the power of life to become more of who we truly are in Christ.

## Cleansing Old Wounds

God wants to cleanse us of the sin that is in us and the sin we do, but He also desires to cleanse us of the wake left behind by the sin that has been done *to* us. We have all experienced wounding at the hands of others when they have either intentionally or unintentionally done harm to us. Children are especially vulnerable any time their parents fall short of perfection, let alone when the adults around them are abusive.

Most importantly, these wounds do not heal without help. Time does not heal, as the old adage claims, it only diminishes our awareness. Nor do we simply "get over it" like so many would have us believe. "Put the past behind you" and "get over it" are in reality toxic euphemisms for repressing painful thoughts and never thinking about them again. But unprocessed pain does not go away. Rather, it will either hound us endlessly or else go underground where it will continue to effect our life without our conscious awareness. Either way it significantly impacts how we live.

Perhaps the most obvious examples of this are the phobias people develop from traumatic experiences. If a young child is bitten by a big dog, they may continue to feel fear around dogs of any size for the rest of their life. And such phobias come in all shapes and sizes. But there are many other types of traumas that are far more damaging.

If a child is criticized in their fumbling attempts to learn new things, they may very well shy away from new experiences, at least when others are around. If a husband is unfaithful to his wife, that betrayal can go so deep that she may never again feel safe in her relationship. When a person causes a serious traffic accident, they may struggle for years with guilt and shame (and some would even say they should!). Wounding happens in many ways and can impact our sense of self for a lifetime. Only the cleansing hand of God can wipe away those painful after-affects. Even then the healing is usually accompanied by one or more additional causes of transformation.

### Releasing Sin, Pain and Trauma

Our part in the cleansing process may involve a great many things, but almost always includes some form of releasing our sin or pain to God. Releasing is not always an easy thing to do, but it is an essential part of being free.

For example, to be washed clean of our anxiety, we must also "cast all our cares upon Him" (1Pet.5:7 PAR). To be fully free of sin, we must confess with our mouth where it is that we need to be cleansed and allow our sin to be nailed to the cross, letting it go. And in order for God to cleanse a wound from the sins of others, we must give Him our pain and suffering.

Releasing is also an *interactive* process. It certainly involves an act of the will, but it would be a mistake to think that it is merely an objective decision and nothing more. Engaging with God for cleansing is a real thing that we actually experience, not simply something we have thoughts about. As God takes away our sin or pain, we sometimes feel physically or emotionally lighter. We might "see" or have a sense of God wiping the slate clean or pulling muck and goo from our soul. Other times we may suddenly feel tired, as if we have put down a heavy load that we had been carrying. In other instances we might not feel the lightness until a few hours or days after our encounter with God.

The point here is that releasing is a real experience, and it is one of the ways in which we are involved in the cleansing process. Deliberately letting go of what is holding us back is an important step in our healing and transformation.

**Summary**

Cleansing is a crucial part of how we become a different person. Sin and wounding from evil need to be removed from our soul, first so that it does not remain part of our identity, and second in order for us to be free enough to become who God created us to be. God never meant for us to be defined by our injuries and failures. He never meant for us to carry the burden of sin and violence the rest of our life. And for those reasons, cleansing is a major part of how we are changed from glory to glory.

## Truth

*Internalizing God's Thoughts and God's Ways*

In one of Paul's most famous statements he assures us that we can be transformed by the renewing of our mind so that we no longer live in ways we learned from our broken world, but instead think and live in ways that are in harmony with the rule and reign of God in our life (Rom.12:2). This includes all of how God sees us, how he views those around us, how he is involved in our life, what matters most, where we need healing and restoration, and how he wants us to give life to others. Some of this comes to us rather quickly on the heels of our conversion. But much of what we need to learn takes more time and requires our mindful pursuit of truth. The following story will hopefully illustrate one way in which renewing our mind through truth can make such a difference.

Much of the healing in my own life has come through revelations of truth that I had already thought about but never really internalized fully. Perhaps the most dramatic of these had to do with the pervasive self-hate I carried around most of my life. I was always quite hard on myself for making mistakes, and yet I had relatively little conscious awareness of my self-hate or how much it permeated every aspect of my life.

For about twenty-seven years I led a reasonably successful career as a software engineer, developing business-level applications and designing software architecture. Nearly everywhere I worked I enjoyed a reputation for being both reliable and capable. Consequently, most of the time I was able to avoid the reality that my self image really was incredibly negative.

During my graduate work at Fuller Seminary, in an effort to earn some income on the side I decided to try my hand at website development, which was as area I had not worked in before. What I discovered was an entirely new world with its own vocabulary, unusual ways of piecing together an application from multiple computer languages, and in many other ways a very different environment than I was familiar with. The differences were so profound that I found myself struggling to accomplish even the most basic necessary coding tasks.

What made this situation even more challenging was the extremely bad quality of the documentation generally available to software developers. It seemed to me as though most of it was written in a way that could only be understood if you had already known what it meant before you began! Even the "tutorials" were frustrating, either because they were too elementary or they skipped too many steps and assumed far too much.

So when I set out to design a web page, I found that I did not even know how to ask my questions in words that seasoned web developers could relate to. Consequently, my searches often turned up nothing of value. If I did find a posting where another person had asked a similar question, the answers would often range from totally irrelevant, to over my head, to very alien discussions between web gurus about the best way to do something. It often took hours or even days for me to accomplish elementary tasks which I could have done in a few minutes in my previous work setting.

Without warning, my deep-seated self-hatred began to emerge and explode. I became unbelievably rageful, screaming at the computer at the top of my lungs, and yelling at the idiots who would not give me a straight answer. Mostly I yelled at myself for not being able to "get it." I had never felt so inadequate in all my life. The whole process of website development was like a massive impenetrable wall, with someone at the top staring down at me and mocking me for my incompetence. There were moments when I seriously doubted my intelligence or my ability to master anything new. I even considered quitting.

One day I simply collapsed from the frustration and rage. It finally dawned on me that something was terribly broken inside, something that had nothing to do with programming at all. So I began talking to God about my desperation, my despair, and my intense rage. For several hours a day, over a period of three days, I sat and wrote furiously in my journal, reviewing every time I could think of where I had felt this way about myself and how it all began. In the process I uncovered numerous experiences from my early life in which I had felt humiliated and stupid. And when I would ask God what he thought about it, he consistently came back with the same few thoughts – He did not see what I saw in those events. In every case, those experiences revealed more about the other people than they did about me. And no one and no event had the right to say who I was except God himself – not even me. While all of that felt true, none of these answers seemed to fully satisfy my feelings of self-hate. And every time I tried to go back to programming, it all came back again.

Finally, on the third day as I sat quietly waiting for God to give me some direction in order to continue our conversation, I felt a strange sensation go through my whole being, like a house of cards collapsing. I could almost see it falling. The thought immediately came to me that self-hate is nothing more than a house of cards – it has no real substance to it at all. Nothing about it is true. At first my reaction was one of disbelief. It seemed impossible to me that such an intractable problem could have no real substance and be so ridiculously false. The dissonance in my head was so pronounced it almost made me dizzy. All I could think was, "It can't be that simple!"

But within a relatively short time I began to feel a great calm, like the quiet after a terrible storm. A great relief began to envelop my mind and heart. I still had doubts about whether I had actually been healed of my self-hate or whether I had slipped into some kind of denial. But those doubts began to dissipate with time as I noticed that day after day would go by without any outbursts of anger or self-deprecating stuff coming out of my mouth. Eventually I came to realize that the collapsing house of cards was God's way of revealing to me the truth about self-hate. It truly is without merit. And that truth got all the way into the depths of my soul and forever changed my sense of self. Truth changed my life.[4]

Jesus once asked his Father to sanctify His disciples with truth (Jn.17:17-19). Or in other words, "transform them little by little over time

4 Note that this is a unique example of inner healing that God tailored for me personally, in part because the symbol was meaningful to me, and healing might look very different for someone else dealing with self-hate.

by means of truth about life in the Kingdom." This is what happens to us when God reveals something to us very directly in such a way that it touches the deepest parts of our heart and mind, changing the way we see and make sense of life, self, and God. These changes can be so profound that we never go back to our previous state of mind.

God can reveal truth to us in a variety of ways. Most commonly, we experience his revelations as spontaneous words, images, or impressions. In the case of my self-hate, he gave me an impression that was almost a physical sensation of collapse, with an image in my mind of a very tall house of cards. Whatever the means, God is able to shape truth in ways that are meaningful to us, so that it "gets in" as it were. This is God writing his laws on our heart (Heb.8:10) so that as we fully digest and internalize His revelations to us, we are changed by the experience and not just educated about our condition.

## Distorted Worldviews

The main reason why truth can be so transformative is because people cannot help but live out of their own worldview. And everyone's worldview has been terribly corrupted and distorted by their own mistaken conclusions about life in our broken world.

Everyone has a worldview – it is not optional. It consists of our collective ideas and assumptions about how life works, both generally and for us personally. This includes our value systems, our ideas about good and evil, our aspirations, our sense of self and others, how we matter, and whatever conclusions we have reached about life from our own experience.

This overall understanding of life then becomes a compass that we use to guide our decisions, evaluate life events, and make sense of our own journey and that of others. But our worldview also operates at a very subconscious level, where it produces many of our emotional reactions to people and events we encounter. How all of this relates to our innate responses is fairly complex, and we cannot hope to sort that all out here. Suffice it to say that our worldview plays a major part in how we react and respond to whatever we experience or think about.[5]

As stated earlier, our worldview does not necessarily correspond very well to reality, and especially not to how life works in the Kingdom of God. In fact, our worldview is extremely suspect at best. The problem is that we have all built the bulk of our worldview out of our own experiences and interpretations of what we see around us. And since we are extremely limited and flawed as human beings, our worldview is full of holes and distortions. That is partly why God can say that His ways are higher than our ways (Isa.55:8-9) and why Paul tells us that we only know part of what there is to know (1Cor.13:12).

Consequently, the more our implicit beliefs are distorted in regard to how life works, the more difficult life will be for us. For example, if my life goal is to reach the top of the corporate ladder and make a six-figure income, I am seriously at risk of missing life altogether – that is, life as God intended. Or if I am convinced that I am defective in some way that makes me less acceptable as a human being, then I will act as if that is true, and what few relationships I have will languish as a result.

Healing and renewing our implicit beliefs about life and our broader worldview will have a direct impact on how we perceive the world around us, how we interpret our perceptions, and how we form our responses to our internal interpretations. Consequently, every aspect of our character is impacted and we live better in spite of our broken world.

### Summary

When God said that his ways are higher than our ways, and his thoughts higher than our thoughts, he was telling us that no matter how smart or

---

5 For more on how to heal our distorted worldviews, see my book *The Truth About Lies and Lies About Truth*.

wise we think we are, we have more to learn about life than we think. His aim in writing his laws on our heart is to help us respond to life out of a renewed heart, much more the way Jesus would. That is why truth is so transforming, once we learn how to let God do the work of revealing truth to us rather than trying to figure things out for ourselves.

What's more, this particular cause for transformation is far more available and accessible than many Christians believe. One reason for this is that we are far more disoriented than we think we are in regard to life in the Kingdom, even when we know a lot of theology. So it is really not very difficult for God to renew our heart and mind by revealing something to us which we have never seen before, or for which we had never seen the kind of significance He places on it. Consequently, change by means of truth can become a very common experience in our walk, as we learn how to spend time in conversation with Him to receive what he has for us. All we need to learn is how to engage with God in ways that allow Him to renew our heart and mind.

## Love

*Being Known, Wanted, and Cared About*

One of our most fundamental needs is to be totally known and loved at the same time by the same person.[6] God designed us for loving relationships, with both himself and with other people. And while it is possible for us to find substitutes for relationship and learn to cope without them, that does not change the truth about what we really need.

To be clear, love here does not refer to sentimentality or fondness we might have for another person. *Love is the will for the good of another, and even extending one's self for the good of another.* When Jesus says, "Love one

6 See Curt Thompson's work on "Being Known".

another," he is not telling us to simply enjoy one another's company; he is commissioning a community of followers who will see to the good of one another and insure that no one is in need of anything that can be provided by their brothers and sisters in Christ.

This is the kind of love that changes who we are. And while there are certain depths of this love we can only experience with God, we also have a deep need for other people who can express this kind of love, however imperfectly. We need to experience being known without condemnation (Rom.8:1), to "feel felt" and matter to one another. Especially in moments when we are most needy, being loved means we are given to and we experience grace and comfort and the loving presence of one who wants to be with us and help us.

In his epic novel, *Les Miserables*, Victor Hugo paints for us an amazing picture of love and its power to transform lives. After the main character Jean Valjean has been reduced to little more than an animal by the French prison system of the eighteenth century, he encounters a bishop who not only feeds him and gives him a place to sleep, but who rescues him from certain death at the hands of the authorities, even after Jean has stolen from the bishop. When the police ask the bishop whether the silver articles do in fact belong to him, the bishop replies that he had given the silver to Jean to keep, but that Jean had forgotten to take the silver candlesticks when he left. Whereupon the bishop hands Jean the additional items. The police have no choice but to release Jean, who is stunned at this grace he has been offerred. In a matter of hours, his life is forever changed by the love he has been shown.

But this kind of love is not limited to fictional novels. We find it on the pages of the New Testament. To be forgiven is an act of love, as the woman who came to Simeon's house and wept over Jesus' feet knew with all her heart. She was moved by love to respond in love. And in the writings of John we get a glimpse of "the disciple Jesus loved" and how much that impacted his life. Perhaps more than any of the other apostles, John "got" how much the love of God matters and how good God is toward us. Paul picks this up as well, especially in his letter to the Ephesians:

> *I pray that you, being rooted and grounded in love, may be able to comprehend with all the saints the breadth and length and height and depth of that love, and know the love of Christ which surpasses knowledge, so that you may be filled up to all the fullness of God (Eph.3:14-19 PAR).*

Paul knew that the more they caught the tremendous extent of God's love for them, the more it would fill them with the presence of God Himself, and the more they would become who God intended for them to be. That is transforming!

In recent years, research into human development has confirmed what God has been telling us for centuries, that our most basic need is to belong, to be bonded in love to another who loves us deeply and cares for our good. Our very identity is formed around our attachments to God and others, so much so that we cannot fully know who we are except in relationship to others with whom we are bonded. Belonging shapes our sense of who we are, whose we are, how we matter, and what is important – all fundamental to our identity as a person.

So when we truly get to know this God who loves us more than we can take in, our soul is able to breathe differently, our mind is able to rest, and our heart is able to trust in ways we could never imagine before. When God begins to heal the brokenness in our life, we find not only relief from pain and suffering, but we discover that God really cares about our pain and is willing to do something about it. When I feel totally alone and discover God's comfort and desire to be with me, I am not only reassured by Him, I feel loved and known by Him and my trust in him grows even stronger.

When He changes my heart to be more loving, more giving, more caring, I am more whole and more who I want to be.

With so much uncertainty in life (and the anxiety that comes from our desire for certainty) we can only live in peace when we have confidence in One who is greater than we are. Being loved grows that kind of trust in us, a trust we cannot produce by willpower or by an affirmation of some propositional truth. Experiencing real love changes who we are.

## Corrective Experiences

*Surprise Encounters with New Ways of Living*

Of all the disciples, Thomas seems to have been the most devastated by the violent death of Jesus. In the space of a single day, all of his aspirations and hopes of the previous three years were destroyed. Nothing could console him, and nothing would convince him that the other disciples had seen anything other than their imaginations gone awry. There was no way to talk him out of his despair.

Then Jesus appears to him and invites him to examine the scars, to see for himself and know for certain – first hand – that his Messiah is alive and well. In that moment, everything changes. Thomas is brought back to life, as it were, from his despair and resignation. He is reborn. He is resurrected with Jesus.

What happened to Thomas might best be referred to as *a corrective experience*. He would have never been talked out of his depression. He could not get past what he had witnessed or his awful conclusion that all was lost. What he needed was another kind of experience, one as powerful as the one that crushed his hope. By his own admission, he needed to see and touch Jesus for himself before he could let himself believe again. Anything else was too painful to consider.

Corrective experiences are wonderfully powerful ways to encounter goodness and truth, sometimes because the experience is entirely new to us, but most often because some aspect of that experience had not yet broken through to our conscious awareness. We may have considered the possibility of such goodness before, yet without much conviction that it could make any difference for us personally. But when we encounter new ways of living or being, the surprise factor can be enough to alter our perceptions of reality and meaning.

Sometime around 1985 when my life had spiraled into a very dark place, I was invited by a friend to attend a support group for people who had experienced the loss of a significant relationship. At first I was quite reluctant to attend, since the group was not expressly Christian in nature. But due to the trust I had in my friend's recommendation, I went anyway.

During one of my first times there, I found myself in a small group of about ten people who had all decided to share their stories that night about how their lives had become unraveled. These were painful stories and hard to listen to without being moved. After one person would finish, a couple of other group members would offer a few words of empathy, usually something like, "That sounds really hard" or "I am so sorry that happened" and even "I have no words … I just feel really sad when I hear your story."

What struck me in that moment was the depth of compassion and soul care that I was witnessing. You have to understand that coming from my background, both family and in certain church settings, the responses of the group members would have been drastically different. Someone might have tried to cheer the person up with a pat answer for their pain. Or worse, told them to get over it, or how to fix it, or why they should not feel so bad. Or worse yet, how it was all their own fault and they had no one to blame for their problems but themselves.

What I saw here was something from another planet entirely. It was soft and caring. People were allowed to feel grief without judgment, to talk about their own mistakes without condemnation, and to speak of injustice without being told what to do. It was truly a sacred space where one could be heard and known and be supported in the middle of a process that would take time for them to sort out and recover from.

After watching this in awe for about an hour, some thoughts began to emerge in my mind that cascaded from one to another. "This is rich! I had no idea people could be this patient and kind with one another. I think I need people like this in my life. It would be really rich to have these kinds of friends!" And then the clincher – "Why don't I know this? I am thirty-four years old, and I don't know that other people could enrich my life? How is this possible?"

It was a corrective experience of the first order. All my life I had considered other people to be mostly problems or difficulties to be dealt with when necessary – occasionally helpful or friendly, but never worth counting on for my deeper needs. Most of the time I believed I was better off alone, and I had plenty of proof to show for it. But here in this moment was irrefutable evidence that I needed people in my life, and they could be good for me. I did not have to be alone.

What a thought! But the fact is that if someone had tried to tell me years earlier that we need one another, I probably would not have believed them, even if I could agree with them in theory that it should be that way. Nothing in my prior experience would have supported the claim that I did not have to be alone or that I might be better off if I was not alone. I needed a corrective experience to show me what I did not know, in order to convince my heart that life could be otherwise.

Now if we had more healthy communities to belong to, we might not have to wait thirty or forty years between corrective experiences. We could encounter these all the time. Especially when coming from any kind of dysfunctional background (which includes most of us), interacting with others who are learning how to receive and give good gifts to one another will change how we see life and how we see ourselves. Even hearing first-hand stories of how people deal with life events from day to day can be quite revealing.

A number of years ago a friend of mine was telling me about a day when she went to the Post Office to mail a package. She put the parcel on the counter and asked how much it would cost to ship. The postal worker took one look at the box and pushed it back toward my friend, scornfully adding, "You can't mail a package like that!"

Without skipping a beat, my friend replied, "Really? You know, I have never been sure what the requirements are for mailing a package. Could you help me out by explaining what I need to do in order to get this ready to mail?" At that point the postal worker became quite helpful and provided the necessary information to my friend, who thanked her and went back home to redo her package.

Believe it or not, I was shocked by what she had done. With my training and background, I would have gone somewhere else! Most likely, I would have either snotted off to the postal worker or else been overwhelmed by shame and quietly removed myself and the package from the building. What my friend had said and done was something that had never occurred to me … ask the other person for their help.

So I asked my friend to tell the story again and explain to me why she did not get angry or shamed or have any of the other reactions that seemed normal to me in that setting. After hearing it a few times, I finally began to see the wisdom and maturity of what she had done.

To this day, when I have to take an item back to a customer service counter, the first words out of my mouth are, "I wonder if you could help me with a problem…?" You would not believe the great service I get. But more importantly, it has helped to remove from my body much of the adversarial stance that I once took with the world around me. And for that reason alone, my friend's story has been for me an incredibly valuable corrective experience.

Once we see this avenue for transformation, it becomes apparent that many people in the Bible had corrective experiences as well, and this perspective helps to shed light on some of the stories we read there. For example, it seems the tax collector Zacchaeus was so shocked when Jesus told him to get dinner ready that it changed his whole life. It was probably the first time in many years he had been given any consideration at all, let alone that someone wanted to come to his home for a meal.

In one of the most moving events of the New Testament, Jesus cooks breakfast for Peter and his friends, and then three times walks him through an affirmation of his love, each time following up with His call on Peter's life. For Peter, this had to be an incredible healing moment, to be restored in such a way after having denied Jesus three times. It was truly a transformative corrective experience.

These moments can be surprisingly powerful and life changing in part because of their surprise factor, and in part because of how our previous life-defeating experiences are best challenged by ones that are life-giving. It is here that we can regain trust that was broken, or discover for ourselves that giving to another can be really joyful, or that restoring a ruptured relationship can be worth the pain and effort.

Perhaps we can summarize corrective experiences this way, that they are *previously unknown options for life, encountered in such a way that they anchor new realities in our body, which in turn transform our sense of what is good and possible, thereby altering our values, our awareness, and our choices.*

We can even create opportunities for corrective experiences. One of the most well-known such examples is that of going on a short-term missions trip. Much of the time, these trips have mixed results in regard to the impact on the people being ministered to. But more often than not, the volunteers return quite changed by their experience. It might be their first exposure to real poverty, or perhaps the greatest effort they have ever put forth for the good of another person. In any case, many of those who go on these trips get more out of it than the people they went to serve. They have created a context that fosters corrective experiences and placed themselves in a position to discover new ways of giving life.

### Corrective Experiences Can Continue Throughout Our Life

Recently I caught a glimpse of something very important that I needed and wanted as a child, though I could not have known at the time what I was missing, only that something was terribly wrong.

While my wife and I were waiting to be seated in a local restaurant, a father and his two children came in and sat in the waiting area with us. The girl, who was perhaps nine, had two pig tails tied with wide blue ribbons, and she had a slight bounce in her step that could only have come from some delight she knew in the depths of her soul. The boy was probably ten or eleven, but unusually calm for a boy his age, walking with a sense of confidence that was in no way self-referenced.

Once they were seated, the girl asked to see her brother's baseball cards, which he gladly produced from his back pocket and handed to her as though they were hers to view for as long as she wanted. He then watched her with joy and satisfaction as she thumbed through the cards and admired his collection. Occasionally she would turn her head and ask a question about a card. As they were talking, one of her ribbons came loose, which she then pulled out the rest of the way and handed to her brother. As if this were a perfectly normal thing to do, she then turned her back to him, and he pulled back her hair and retied the ribbon for her. It was a simple and quiet gesture, a beautiful picture of two children who lived with a secure sense of being together.

These were such unremarkable actions, yet it was all I could do not to weep. It was a portrait of love, of shared experiences, and of joy they drank in as if it were normal to be cared about and to care. So this is what it looks like to be a child in a real family! To have a brother or sister who wants to be with you, and with whom you want to be.

I could not help but wonder, as I watched, what kind of father this was and what manner of man and woman could raise children such as these? As if to answer my question, the two children moved with ease a bit closer to the place where their father sat, and he pulled his son onto his lap, wrapping his arm around him in order to hold the baseball cards his daughter handed to him as she snuggled up on his other side. And in that posture they went though the cards again, one at a time, and talked among themselves.

I can still replay that video in my mind today, watching in awe as they engage each other in their graceful dance of love and joy. What must it feel like to be that boy or that girl? How does it feel to be so secure in who you are and whose you are at such a young age?

For a moment I can almost feel the edge of it, but never the whole – it seems too big, and I have very little inside me that can grab hold of what it means. How every touch, every look, every thought could be so good and so common at the same time for all of them. To this day, this continues to be for me a recurring corrective experience.

## Retraining

*Forming New Pathways in Our Mind and Body*

The Apostle Paul often talked about our need for training. He personally mentored Timothy and many other early Christians. One of his best known statements about sacred writings include a reference to the value of training: "*All Scripture is inspired by God and is profitable for teaching, for reproof, for correction, for training in righteousness; so that a person of God may be adequate, equipped for every good work*" (2Tim.3:16-17). But unless we are careful, we can gloss over this term and assume Paul is talking about being trained in how to study the Word or how to participate in a church ministry. Such a view would seriously miss some of the most important tools for spiritual formation.

We all have our own style or personality which has been formed over time through complex interactions between our natural inborn traits and the social context in which we live. This interaction is so tightly woven together that the old nature-nurture debate has largely been retired in favor of more balanced theories of human development in which each effects the other. And this process of impacting our environment even as we are being changed by it begins so early in life that it is almost impossible to determine how it is that we have become the person we are at any given moment.

When people say, "That's just who I am" they usually mean something like, "My way of feeling and acting is hard-wired into my brain, and there is no point in trying to pretend it can be any different." But barring some unusual neurological issues, this is almost never the case. The truth is that we have been formed in thousands of small ways which we are not even aware of as we are acquiring various skills and attitudes. Growing up in poverty, for example, could train a person to be vigilant about every scrap of food or useful matter, whereas growing up in affluence could train a person to be cavalier about such things and able to toss food in the garbage without a care and find something else that better suits their taste buds. We are also trained in such things as gratitude versus ingratitude, racism versus acceptance, pride versus humility, and so on.

By the time we are old enough to reflect on our own values, it feels like we have felt that way forever, that we were born with those values, and we have almost no sense of having been significantly shaped into the person we are through interacting with other people. The relationship between nature and nurture is simply too complex to sort out.

The good news is that this has tremendous implications for spiritual formation. In short, it means that our soul is really quite malleable. If we have been trained in a particular manner that is unhealthy or self-defeating, we can also be retrained in in ways that will alter those feelings and attitudes and behaviors. We can become different on the inside by choosing to be trained in ways that are more life-giving.

One of the most simple yet powerful examples of this can be seen in regard to practicing *appreciation and gratitude*. We have witnessed the impact of this basic practice many times in recent years. At the end of each day, you take a few minutes to recount those things from the day that you appreciate. At a minimum, you attempt to find at least one thing in each of five main categories:

1. What do I appreciate about my day, generally?
2. What do I appreciate about another person?
3. What do I appreciate about myself?
4. What do I appreciate about God?
5. What do I think God appreciates about me or about this day?

If more than one thing comes to mind in an area, that is even better. Some people make it a practice to find three things in each area, and call it their "three-by-five" appreciation. For the greatest impact, this should be done out loud with another person or written in a journal or emailed to a friend.

After practicing this for a few weeks, most people are surprised to discover that they are becoming more grateful and positive in their overall outlook on life. They begin to see more good in their life and more of God's involvement as well. They even begin to *expect* to see more good in their day to day experience. That is because they are retraining their mind to focus on what it good, and that in turn begins to reshape their inner being.

Another practice we call *bookends* helps us to grow our sense of the goodness of God. As you drift off to sleep at night and as you wake up in the morning, turn your thoughts to the goodness of God for just five or ten minutes. Consider His love, the quality of His character, His generosity, and the like. That is it. We call it *bookends*, because we use this practice to bracket our day, like bookends. Although this might seem like a rather trivial practice, most people find that in a few weeks they begin to look for and expect to see the goodness of God in their life in ways they had not done before. They are retraining their mind to be aware of and anticipate goodness in new ways.

These are two examples of a more general case of what is commonly referred to as *spiritual practices* or *spiritual disciplines*. Generally, these kinds of practices are things we can do that are within our ability, which over time will alter our bodies and minds in ways that we could not have accomplished by any direct effort or act of the will.[7] It is not unlike the ways in which we train ourselves to play tennis, drive a car, or do any number of things more or less out of habit and with very little conscious thought, once we are well trained.

This should not be confused with a "fake it 'till you make it" approach to change. We are not pretending to be something we are not or claiming to have an ability or attitude we do not have. We are simply engaging in a practice that will retrain our internal systems, so that our default reactions and responses to life are changed.

Many people are turned off by spiritual practices due to the possibility of them becoming legalistic or because they tried some practices in the past that dried up and lost their value over time. But what we need to know is that we also have to be trained in *how* to use spiritual practices for training. This is not something that is immediately obvious, because the process involved runs counter to how we normally accomplish things in the world.

The important thing to grasp is that spiritual practices do not create life or bring about change merely by engaging in them. Rather, their primary

7 This is roughly Dallas Willard's definition of spiritual disciplines.

purpose is to create a context within which we can engage with God in some unique manner. It is engaging with God that changes us.

For example, I could practice appreciation as an exercise in list-making, trying to see how many good things I can add to the list. But doing so will probably not do much for my spiritual life. On the other hand, if I search my heart and allow myself to genuinely appreciate the gifts that come to me each day, thanking God for all He has offered me, then it will most likely impact my soul. If I go on a silent retreat and sit for hours with no thoughts in my head at all, my primary benefit will probably be that of stress relief. However, if I use the silence to reach out to God and feel His presence with me and to listen to His voice, I may well be changed significantly by the end of my retreat.

Given that a number of authors have covered this area well, I will not spend much more time on this aspect of spiritual transformation. Suffice it to say that tens of thousands of Christians over many centuries have found these practices to be a highly accessible means of forming their character to be more like Jesus.

For the purposes of our model, we will define retraining as *a process of being mentored and directed into a variety of experiences that stretch our soul and expose our defects, transforming our ability to respond well in more complex circumstances, thereby altering our options for responding to life.*

## Authentic Relationships

*Bonding With Other People of Character*

Recent decades have seen tremendous progress in our understanding of the human brain and how it is designed. Among other things, this research has powerfully reinforced something that the biblical writers knew a long time ago about human nature. Which is, that God designed us for relationship.

So much so, that it might be said that *relationship is the organizing principle of life* as God intended.

Not only are we designed for attachment and bonding, these bonds then contribute greatly to our character formation and our ability to grow and mature as human beings. For it is within these bonded relationships that we develop our sense of being and well-being,[8] form our sense of trust, grow our capacity for emotional distress, experience some of life's deepest joys and sorrows, and become who we are in thousands of tiny ways that would be too numerous to describe.

Consequently, the character of those we bond with is intricately and intimately tied to our own spiritual, emotional, and psychological health. If we bond as an infant or child to emotionally wounded or disabled care-givers, we will internalize significant problems that will need God's healing and restoration later on. And if we find genuinely good people to bond with later in life, those connections can bring about some of the important changes we need in our heart and mind.

Relationships are so foundational to who we are that our attachment patterns and our bonding experiences will literally alter how our mind works, both neurologically and functionally.[9] This is why learning how to build an authentic, tangible relationship with God can be so life-changing, in and of itself. This is also why we need to seek out and develop authentic friendships and healthy connections with others. The people we bond with matter a great deal to our own personal development.

During the first thirty-some years of my life, my primary approach to dealing with the narcissists around me was to morph into whatever it was they needed or wanted from me at any given moment. While that tended to minimize their emotional assaults on me, this strategy (which was mostly

---

8 The terms "sense of being" and "well-being" are borrowed from Leanne Payne's work.

9 See Curt Thompson's, *Anatomy of the Soul* for a complete analysis.

running below the conscious level) had the terrible side-effect of causing me to lose myself almost entirely. By the time I was in my mid-thirties, I had no idea who I was or how I mattered. Those relationships had all but destroyed my sense of being, my hope, and my relational capacities. It has only been through new relationships that I have been able to repair the damage done by those early connections, and rebuild my sense of self and my ability to relate better to others.

Of course, much of this has been in concert with the other causes of transformation as well. But it would be hard to measure the extent of change I have experienced simply by virtue of being bonded to far healthier people. While I still deal with many remnants of my earlier malformation, I am a significantly different person today than I was at thirty-four. And much of that change I attribute directly to the good people in my life, especially my wife, Jan. If it were not for them, I would not be writing a book on transformation.

One of the great myths among many Christians is the belief that "all I need is Jesus and me." Somehow we get the idea that since everyone around us is flawed, we do not need them in our life. But the truth is that our lack of good bonding can be as dangerous to our health as the toxic bonding we do have. Learning how to nurture authentic relationships with imperfect people is part of what builds our character in the first place. But more than that, we truly need authentic bonds in order to be fully human and fully who God intends for us to be.

"Love one another" is not simply an order to be obeyed. The reason it was given as the second greatest commandment is because it is so foundational to who God designed us to be. We were created as relational beings who need God and other people as much as we need air and water. Being bonded to God impacts our heart and mind as surely as a furnace will purge out the impurities from raw ore. And in similar fashion, we are also changed by building authentic relationships with other people of character.

## Summary

As can be seen from this overview, God has given us multiple direct causes for transformation, of which these six are the most common and probably the most significant. Identifying these primary sources leads us to several important conclusions.

First, God has provided many points of intervention to get us started again when we are stuck. One person might need a corrective experience in order to wake up to what God wants for them. Another might be struggling because of a faulty understanding of life and need God's truth to break through the fog and set them free. Still another could be dealing with the after-affects of abandonment and need love that can breathe new life into their famished soul.

When we think about it, it only makes sense that God would offer us life-changing gifts tailored for every human and spiritual need. We are all broken, but in different ways and due to many different life experiences. God has answers for all of them. From that perspective alone we would expect to find multiple causes for transformation and restoration.

Second, having multiple avenues for change means we have far more possibilities for experiencing growth and renewal on a daily basis. Following Jesus is not meant to be a test to pass or a standard to try to live up to. Apprenticeship is a life of "being transformed into the same image from one degree of glory to another" (2Cor.3:18) as a matter of course. Thus, transformation is not a rare or elusive experience, but the stuff of daily life with God. And one of the reasons this is possible is because there are multiple ways in which we can be impacted for good.

Third, given such vast resources for change, we are challenged to learn more about how to participate well with all that God has for us. Much of the Christian world today is still tied to the idea that Christianity is a lifestyle that we have to aspire to and try hard to emulate. The resulting performance-driven approach to discipleship is a proven failure for lasting change. Only when we give up our efforts to change ourselves, and instead learn how to participate with what God has provided, will there be any hope of reviving our churches and our people.

That brings us to our next topic, which is to understand the primary factors involved in effective participation for change.

# Chapter 3
# Our Participation

Recognizing that all of the causes for transformation come from God and others does not mean we have nothing to do with the process. Quite the opposite. Transformation requires our conscious participation with God and others as we learn how to engage with these various causes for change. If you think about it, this only makes sense. Becoming more like Jesus obviously means some aspect of our character is changing and we are beginning to live differently in some particular area than we did previously. We are involved, by definition.

When you go to the doctor for help, you are intimately involved in the healing process. You consent to the examination. You stand up or lay down as required. You submit to tests. You hold out your arm and allow nurses to stick needles into it, then you take care not to pull them out accidentally. As part of your treatment, you may have to alter your diet, take certain medications, and set aside time for more meetings with the doctor. You are involved all the time, every step of the way.

In similar fashion, we need to learn how to participate with God so He can do in us what we cannot do for ourselves. That is what it means to receive grace as a Christian.

## The Trouble with Participation

Unfortunately, this is where Christians seem to have the most trouble. In fact, some of the greatest problems Christians have faced since the beginning of the New Covenant have been in regard to how we are meant to participate in our own spiritual development. The Galatians got it wrong, the medieval church nearly destroyed our grasp of it, and most of our modern Christian organizations are deeply mistaken about how this works.

In a nutshell, the main problem today is an over-reliance on willpower, which is clearly visible in various performance-based, try-harder approaches to Christian development. Or to put it bluntly, much of the Church is heavily committed to legalistic imitations of spiritual growth.

Most of us have thought about legalism as a problem that some other group has, because they have a lot more rules about what they can and cannot do. But that is only the tip of the iceberg. Legalism is actually a belief and practice that relies on willpower and motivation to try as hard as we can to do the things we are supposed to do as good Christians. We may profess a reliance on the Holy Spirit, but the truth is that most of our efforts are simply human-based attempts to do what we think are the "right" things to say and do.

Take the common experience we have all had of a head/heart split. In my head I know I should forgive some person who has betrayed my trust, but in my gut it feels like what they have done is unforgivable. Suppose I decide to be "obedient" and squelch my emotions to where I can barely feel my resentment, and then screw up my willpower so I can write a letter to this person and tell them, "I forgive you." I may even congratulate myself on "getting the victory" over my flesh.

But in order to go down that road, I have to ignore a big neon sign that is trying to get my attention. Because what I have actually done is to imitate forgiveness without ever really having formed a forgiving heart. In essence, I managed to "clean the outside of the cup" by saying "I forgive you" while by-passing the process of cleaning up my heart so that I truly care for and want what is good for the other person. Convincing myself that I am being obedient because I said the words is an exercise in self-deception and self-righteousness. Forgiveness is not just an act, it is a condition of the heart toward another.

This is, in essence, an example of a *failure to participate* in an authentic process of transformation, substituting willpower and self-motivation in its place in order to produce a desired outcome. Unfortunately, most of us have grown so accustomed to this way of proceeding that this has now become the most common approach to dealing with spiritual dynamics.

### Participating Well

Learning how to participate well in our own spiritual development is very different from trying to "apply" all the good things we read in the Bible or talk about in church. For starters, we need to aim at very different goals than what most of us have been taught. Rather than trying to do what seems to be the right things to do, we need to first become the kind of person from whom good things come by nature. That way we live out of who we are, instead of always trying to override who we are. We will not get very far by trying to *act* more like Jesus. We need to *become* more like Jesus, taking on more of His character. Only then will we begin to live more the way He lived.

This is the way of transformation.

As we learn how to participate with God and others to change who we are on the inside, our outer life will also change by virtue of who we are becoming. Good fruit comes from a good tree. That is the nature of things. We can only genuinely live out of who we are on the inside. Anything else is an effort to be something we are not.

In the sections to follow, we will examine several of the most significant aspects of participating well. But by way of an overview, it is important to keep in mind that transformation is very much an indirect process. We cannot produce a change of character by direct effort, any more than we can add a foot to our height through an act of our will. Change comes from an indirect process with which we can learn how to participate.

A good metaphor of participation can be seen in farming. If our intention is to produce corn, we start by plowing, planting, fertilizing, weeding, and watching. Most of the real work is done by rain, sunlight, air, and nutrients from the soil. We have no way of producing corn by any direct means, such as smashing together amino acids. Instead, we have to *participate* with how nature works, and in the process reap a harvest of corn. Jesus put it this way:

> *The kingdom of God is like a man who casts seed upon the soil; and he goes to bed at night and gets up by day, and the seed sprouts and grows, how, he himself does not know. The soil produces crops by itself; first the blade, then the head, then the mature grain in the head (Mk.4:26-28).*

Producing food is done by very indirect means. That is what makes it the perfect illustration of spiritual growth. In another place, Jesus used the image of grapes and a grapevine to make the same point. We cannot produce fruit by trying to make fruit. We produce fruit by connecting to the vine (Jn.15).

A similar image can be seen in sailing. Rather than trying to move the boat by direct means, such as rowing, our efforts are focused on aligning the sails and rudder, participating with the wind and water in ways that cause the boat to move forward.

So it is with transformation. We cannot change our heart or character by an act of our will or any other direct means. And trying to do so will eventually lead to despair and the belief that real change is impossible. But if we learn how to participate with the Holy Spirit and the various resources God has given to us, our inner life will change in ways we would otherwise have no access to at all. It is the indirect process that makes the difference.

With that as a context for how we are involved in the process, let us look more closely at some of the most important aspects of participation.

## Relentless Intentionality

*Focused and Purposeful Attention*

It has been said that at least one set of stairs to the temple was intentionally made to be very irregular in both depth and height, so that people could only approach the temple in a mindful manner, paying attention to each step along the way. What a beautiful metaphor – that getting close to God requires focused and deliberate steps. We do not get there by being absent-minded or indifferent to the process. The same can be said about almost anything good or meaningful that we want to bring to fruition in our broken world.

For much of our life, our character is formed by a fairly haphazard and random process. The fact is, we are being formed spiritually all the time – for good or ill – by everything we see, everything we do, everything we think about, things that happen to us, and even by the absence of some good things that we should have experienced but did not. Which means that spiritual formation is not optional. It is not something we can choose to opt out of if we are not interested. We are always being formed into the person we are at any given moment, and we will continue being formed into whatever sort of person we will become. This is largely an indirect process, as discussed above, but it is going on all the time.

This leads us to the important truth that one of our most important tasks as apprentices of Jesus is to learn how to *intentionally* pursue those things that will shape us more and more into the person God intends for us to be. We may not be able to change who we are by *direct* means, but what we can do is actively engage with God and others in appropriate contexts and with useful practices that will then shape us in ways we want to be formed. This is the path that leads to the abundant life we read about in the New Testament. But to do so requires a very intentional strategy, because transformation rarely happens by accident.

### Our Innermost Being

Before going much further, one more thing needs to be made very clear. It ought to go without saying, but too many people seem to bypass this important step. First and foremost, we must understand that *every one of us actually has an inner life that can change and grow far more than we realize, and thus we can be transformed over time.*

The reality that we possess such a malleable character does not seem to be something of which people are generally aware. Perhaps this stems from social demands and expectations which keep us preoccupied to the extent that we rarely notice how we are being shaped and formed. But the indirectness of the process itself is likely most responsible for our inability to see how this all works. When someone asks us why we think or feel as we do about certain things, we often shrug our shoulders and say, "That's just who I am." Our character formation is such an indirect process, we are often unaware of *how* it is happening and even the fact *that* it is happening at all. Our intuitive sense is that we are who we are, simply because that is who we are! Only rarely do most people grasp how much they have been formed and malformed by a process, one in which they were deeply involved, but mostly at a subconscious level.

What this means is that our character and our very sense of who we are as a person are far more pliable than we might believe. We do not become an angry or fearful or bitter person by some accident of birth or genetics (except in fairly rare cases). We form those attributes over time through thousands of interactions with people and the world around us. And this applies to virtually any character trait we might have, desirable or not.

In the end, this is incredibly good news! Because whatever character we have today can change and become different. Once we decide to be intentional about our formation, we can begin to engage with God and others in ways that will reform our thoughts, feelings, dispositions, and nearly everything else about our character to become more and more like that of Jesus Himself.

The key to change, however, is held in the fact that the process is so indirect. Which, first of all, explains why our direct efforts to change do not accomplish much, even though most teaching today on Christian living assumes that it *should* work. But second, the fact that this process is indirect will point us in a different direction for a truly effective approach to transformation, an issue that we will take up again later on.

### Necessary Change

Not only are we *capable* of change, but we are desperately *in need* of change. This has to be said explicitly, because people today are becoming much more resistant to personal challenges or moral imperatives that would suggest their souls are in disrepair. Apart from a more fragile sense of self that now seems to be the norm, perhaps the greatest reason for this is that the world is rapidly loosing any distinction between feelings and truth. Feelings are now taken to be the proper basis for all discernment, values, and meaning. To suggest that a person needs change or that we need to submit to God in order to find life is now looked upon as a form of intolerance or even hate speech. People often consider themselves to be above reproach, with an absolute right to remain as they are, unanswerable to anything beyond their own feelings of satisfaction. They might even be offended at the idea that their very nature has been formed over time, and is not "just the way they are."

This kind of self-imposed spiritual deafness of course is serious enough to keep anyone immature or create a narcissistic culture. Our only hope for becoming more whole is to grasp how far we really have fallen short of the person God created us to be, and then to actively and intentionally engage in the process of healing and growing in the hope of becoming more and more our true self. Because unless we want to become different than we currently are and are willing to take the necessary steps to move in that direction, we will continue to be shaped by forces we cannot see, with no way to predict who it is that we will become. Thank God, that Jesus came to save us from ourselves!

Change is both possible and necessary. Our only hope for an abundant life as seen in the New Testament is to intentionally change the means by which we are being formed. Only then will we become the kind of people who can live in the Kingdom the way God meant for us to live.

**Proper Use of Our Will**

It is this *intentional* refocusing of our effort and learning that constitutes a proper use of our will. Just as a farmer can choose to plant certain particular seeds and nurture the growing plants to produce a crop he could never create directly, so also we can choose to participate in our formation in order to grow spiritually, eradicate evil from our soul, and become more loving toward others. We cannot produce these qualities by direct effort, but we can use our will to redirect our spiritual formation. Our will is the means by which we choose to become apprentices of Jesus and commit ourselves to a life of learning how to live. This is what it means to participate well. Notice the intentionality reflected in the following verses:

> *Seek the Lord while he may be found; call upon him while he is near (Isa.55:6).*

> *Ask and it shall be given to you; seek and you will find; knock and it will be opened to you (Mt.7:7).*

Jesus has everything we need to learn from Him and receive from Him as His disciples, and He invites us to come to Him and engage with Him for all that He has to offer.

In saying this, we need to be clear that we are speaking of an interactive relationship with God, not religious activity. Most of us have been taught that "doing things for God" is how we show our love for Him, and that if we try hard enough, our heart will catch up in the end. Not only is this idea dangerously close to "God helps those who help themselves," this performance-driven approach completely distorts the Christian life. In order to be a disciple, we have to engage with our Teacher so we can become more like Him (Lk.6:40). This interactive relationship is crucial to our formation. Without it we are simply following guidelines, not a real person.

So what does it look like to be more intentional? For starters, it means that we find other people who are further along on this path and learn from them. Being an apprentice is far more than an education or a set of tasks. It is an experiential student-to-teacher relationship that most of us need to be mentored in, or we will not know where to begin.

More than anything else, this means we devote ourselves to learning as much as we can about how to participate well in this process. Our aim is to learn how to actively look for and engage in the various means of transformation, including truth, love, cleansing, corrective experiences, retraining, and authentic relationships. Some of this will take place in moments of solitude with God, and some of this will require the participation of a larger life-giving community. Virtually all of it will involve being purposeful and intentional about where we focus, what we do, and how we proceed.

## Radical Receptivity

*Surrendering and Submitting to the Work of God*

Given that God is the source of the primary means for transformation, and we are the recipients of these gifts, it only makes sense that we would learn how to receive well! All the things that bring about transformation including cleansing, truth, love, corrective experiences, and retraining, all come from outside of us. None of those means will impact us unless we learn how to receive them fully.

One of Jesus' most famous parables, the one about the farmer planting seeds, addresses this issue of receptivity very directly. In the parable, there are four types of soil upon which the farmer cast his seeds, which Jesus referred to as hard, rocky, thorny, and good. When the ground was hard, it failed to apprehend the seeds at all; they were picked off by the birds and the ground never benefited in any way. The rocky ground initially received the seeds gladly, but never let them take root well enough to make a difference when life got hard. In other words, they liked to hear what Jesus had to say, but they never internalized what He said. The ground covered with thorns had still another problem, in that it was deeply divided between good seed and weeds. In time the weeds choked out the life-giving plants.

Only the good soil received the seeds in full and allowed the roots to go deep enough to make a difference. The ground was prepared for what needed to happen, and the seeds grew up into a fruitful harvest. In a word, this soil was receptive in a way that the other soils were not. And that receptivity made all the difference in the world.

Most importantly, receptivity means that transformation is not an achievement, but something we receive. This distinction is crucial. Only when we understand our desperate need for outside intervention in our soul will we begin to see our incredible need to be given something that we ourselves do not possess. In more theological terms, this is our need for *grace* – for God to do in us and for us what we cannot do on our own.

If intentionality is all about how we choose the path that leads to life, then receptivity is our primary avenue to becoming what we have chosen. Jesus had a lot to say about receptivity. "Let those who have ears to hear, listen, and those who have eyes to see, perceive what I have said to you" (Mk.4:9,12).

**Missing the Point**

Unfortunately, one of the single greatest problems facing Christians today is the pervasive belief that if we try hard to do the right things, the Holy Spirit will give us the strength to do them. This myth is believed and taught by some of the leading theologians of our day.[10] They may quote a lot of verses about how God is responsible for sanctification, but they then go on to quote verses which command us to "obey" in order to grow. From this apparent dual process they come to the conclusion that if we do what we can, then God will supply what we are missing.

However, Paul says the exact opposite, that if you try really hard to do the right things you will come to the end of yourself (Rom.7). Spiritual growth does not come from trying hard to live up to some standard. It is a work that God does in us. Transformation has to do with first changing what is inside us, so that what comes out of us is different that what it otherwise would have been. Making our behavior the starting point for God's intervention is completely backwards, and stands all of the New Testament teaching on its head.

> *"First clean the inside of the cup, so that the outside also may become clean" (Mt.23:26).*

What seems to be the point of confusion here is the term "obedience." Somehow in our minds this word gets connected with "performance" before we ever have a chance to think about what it really means. Once that connection gets established, it immediately blossoms into a question of "what to do" in order to produce the right outcomes. This in turn distorts our understanding of discipleship, which then affects nearly everything we believe about what it means to grow spiritually.

God never meant for us to confuse *obedience* with *compliance.* Behind this performance-driven approach to the Christian life is an unspoken

10 Dieter, et al, *Five Views on Sanctification*

presupposition, that a disciple is one who acts like Jesus. But that puts the cart before the horse, as it were. The truth is, a disciple is one who is devoted to learning how to *become* like their Teacher. That is, how to take on the character and quality of their Master, so they can then live more the way He does.

The reason why discipleship has been such a train wreck during the last century is because we have been trying to get people to do things without having first been transformed into the kind of person who has the character to live the way Jesus said.

A common example is that of trying to forgive someone of a serious offense. When the offended person says, "I don't think I can ever forgive them for what they did," their mentor might respond with something like, "You need to repent of that unforgiveness and forgive them anyway." Or to put it another way, "It does not matter how you feel about this. You need to do the 'right' thing, which is to screw up your courage and willpower and act like you have forgiven them."

But here is an important question. If I have to use my willpower to override my heart, what does that say about the condition of my heart? And if forgiveness is really a heart condition more than an action, have I truly forgiven the person or simply imitated forgiveness? In reality, the only thing that has changed is that I have deluded myself into thinking I have been obedient when in reality I have totally dodged it!

If anything, this should begin to unmask the truth, which is that most of the evangelical emphasis on "obedience" has actually produced its very antitheses. We simply cannot do by our own direct effort the sort of things Jesus said and did. Once we get this, we can step back and begin to rethink what the New Testament might mean when it talks about obedience. At that point the whole process of discipleship takes on new meaning, as we see how obedience has a lot more to do with being a good student than it has to do with performing well. Learning from Jesus how to become a good person in His Kingdom will change everything else about our life and behavior.

Which brings us back to *receiving* as a major part of what it means to participate in transformation. But since we have all grown up in a highly individualistic, achievement-oriented culture, learning how to receive is a lot harder than it looks. Most of our training in this world is based on how to *achieve* what we want through hard work. Even our idea of what it means to be a student is wrapped up in the achievement terminology of grades and degrees. All of which makes it challenging for us to switch gears and learn how to receive what we need in order to become more the person God created us to be. What does receiving look like? How are we involved? How do we proceed? These are not trivial problems.

### Receptivity is Not Passive

For starters, it is important to note that the opposite of achieving is not passivity. The opposite of today's dominant understanding of obedience is neither license nor laziness. Being receptive is an interactive, highly engaged process of allowing God to do in us what we are unable to do for ourselves. Learning to participate in receiving is at the very core of transformation.

Going back to the metaphor of farming, it is anything but passive. Yet the harvest is never achieved by direct effort. Rather it is the indirect result of a different kind of work entirely. The farmer does not make corn, he plants seeds, irrigates, weeds, and so forth, and in the end he "receives" a harvest of corn he could never produce by direct effort or an act of the will. But notice how much real effort goes into the process of creating a context for the result!

This illustrates an important spiritual principle. The work God does in us (that is, grace) is not opposed to effort; it is only opposed to earning or achieving what God provides.[11] An apprentice of Jesus has much to do in

11 Credit goes to Dallas Willard for this important observation.

order to participate in the necessary training, but they do not try to produce the desired outcomes directly.

In the earlier example of trying to forgive a person for something that felt unforgivable we showed how direct effort failed to produce genuine forgiveness. But suppose instead the apprentice goes to Jesus and wrestles with Him regarding the condition of his heart and his anger and desire for justice. As Jesus heals his emotional injury and reveals to him more of God's perspective, the person's pain is diminished, his resistance loses ground, and his consideration for the other person grows into a desire for their healing and restoration. At some point in this process, the apprentice truly desires to forgive the offender, in order for them both to be more free, and because he has already been changed to have a forgiving heart toward the other.

In short, he has received something from God he could not do for himself – a change of heart. Still nothing about the process was passive. Grace requires our participation, and especially our receptivity. We often think that if the other person would change, we would forgive them. But it turns out that we ourselves are the ones who need to change in order to forgive. And for that change to happen, we need to engage with God so He can do a work in us that is beyond our ability. That is part of what it means to be an apprentice of Jesus.

### Being Teachable

Receptivity is also about being more teachable. This is because God's thoughts and ways are so much different than our ways, and there is much more to learn about life in the Kingdom than we know. And the kind of training we need is not just about doctrine or ideas of the Christian life, but rather is experiential in nature and comes from engaging with God directly, learning by practice and involvement in the work of God with us.

An excellent example of receptivity can be seen in Psalm 139. Here the psalmist invites God to search his heart and reveal whatever might be there that needs healing or transformation. "Search me O God and know my heart and my thoughts. See if there is any hurtful way in me, and lead me in the way everlasting." He is like a man standing under a spotlight with arms outstretched, saying, "Let's do this, God! Let's get rid of whatever You can find in here that is not good."

Notice first, his tremendous trust. He knows that exposing his heart to God is not only safe, it is in his best interests to do so, no matter what might be in there. God is good, and God will be good to his heart. He knows he is desperately needy for what God has for him, and he is putting his whole life on the line for that purpose.

Second, notice how involved he is. His intention is apparent in his proactive approach to God, and his request for help is evidence of his willingness to receive. The mood of the entire psalm is one of reflection and contemplation of who he is, who God is, how dependent he is, and so on. And he deliberately engages with God for what he needs.

Third, observe his total honesty and transparency before God. That takes work, because we are prone to ignore our faults and inner flaws at the expense of self-honesty. Taking the time to examine our heart with God can open up avenues of healing and restoration we did not even know we needed. But it does not usually come very easily. Participating fully with our Mentor means leveling with Him about who we really are.

A great illustration of teachability comes from the famous psychiatrist, M. Scott Peck, who says our internal worldview is much like a map that we use to navigate life.[12] The problem, he says, is that most of us have a messed up map which does not work nearly as well as we think it does. So we keep running into dead ends, getting lost, and being frustrated with how things work out day to day. And what makes this even more frustrating is our dedication to the map as it is, regardless of how often it fails us. We keep blaming the world around us instead of doing the work necessary to revise

12 See M. Scott Peck, *The Road Less Traveled (first part of book).*

our map. In some cases we might even need to tear up major portions of the map and start over. That is what it looks like to be teachable and malleable.

Sometimes, though, our religious commitments get in the way. We may believe that because our doctrine is "pure" and our commitment to the Bible is unwavering, that we mostly know whatever it is we need to know and our only problem is in trying to apply the Word and work it out in our life. But that assumes way too much. In truth, our internal map of life is far more distorted than we think, despite whatever theological training we might have had. And unless we are open to change, we will continue fighting the same fights over and over, getting the same results.

**Surrender**

Combining this broad understanding of receptivity with what was said earlier about intentionality, a powerful new definition for *surrender* begins to emerge. Surrendering ourselves to God is the very essence of what it means to be a Christian. This element is so important, Paul uses the image of death and resurrection to emphasize how significant it is. We die to our old life and are resurrected to our new life in Christ. "You are not your own, you were bought with a price." Surrender could not be any more complete.

Now to some extent, we all struggle with total surrender. For example, anyone who has been abusively controlled by another may find the idea of surrender to be almost intolerable, which is truly understandable. They have had to fight for an identity of their own, to be able to breathe on their own without being told what to do. Talk of surrender can feel like a death sentence with no good outcome on the other side.

Another person may struggle with surrender purely on the grounds of their desire to run their own life without interference from God or anyone else. Even those who are willing to give much of their life to God usually have little spaces in their world where they would like to remain in control.

Of course, this is part of what God wants to save us from, since we were never designed to live that independently from Him.

In any case, whatever we might feel in regard to surrendering our heart and mind and body to God, that resistance is just more evidence of how much we need His healing and restoration. Total trust in God is what we were made for, however strange that may sound or feel. That is the reality of who God is and what He had in mind when He created the world.

The point is that when we uncover any resistance in our self to total surrender, we can begin to see how much we need to be *intentional* about our *receptivity* to God in order for us to come to the place where we will want to give up our life to Him more fully. These two areas go hand in hand for every step we take toward renewal and transformation.

**Receptivity is Relational**

Above all, receiving is relational. As our interactive relationship with God continues to develop over time, we receive Life (with a capital "L") from God in ways we could never imagine apart from Him. God loves us beyond our wildest dreams, and He desires to give His children every good spiritual gift we might need. He is a generous God, and wants to do for us what we cannot do on our own.

Christians who have been taught that most of the work is up to them often get the sense that God is not involved much at all. It may be hard for them to believe God can do anything in their heart that will make a difference. If they hear a call to become more generous, they are able to sit down and work out a budget for giving a little more to a good cause, and their reason for doing so may be out of duty or to out of obedience to what God requires. It never occurs to them that God wants to give them a heart of generosity so they can literally rejoice over the chance to make a difference in the life of another person.

Imagine for a moment how two young people in love cannot wait to give good things to each other, to surprise each other with joy, and to encourage the life they feel between them. That is only a glimpse of how much God wants to be with us, to love us, and to give us what we need for healing, for growth, and for life itself.

But we need to learn how to receive. God never runs over our desires or forces His gifts upon us. He wants a *relationship* with us, which means we have to respond to Him and receive what He has for us. There is no other way, no other substitute. We cannot act as if we have received something we have not. Nor can we pretend we do not need to receive in order to be a "good Christian." Building a relationship with God that is tangible, real, and interactive is vital to our ongoing restoration. It is within that connection with Him that we draw the life we need in order to be transformed.

**Summary**

Receiving from God is a learned process. It does not come naturally to us. Seeking Him out, growing in relationship with Him, finding out what He has for us and how He wants to do His work in our heart – these all require our persistent attention and our deliberate pursuit of Him.

But once we get the hang of it we begin to discover how vast His riches toward us truly are! We begin to encounter more cleansing, truth, love, corrective experiences, mentoring, and life from relationship than we ever thought possible. May we all learn how to receive more!

## Restorative Practices

*Making Wise Use of Spiritual Practices*

Saints all through history have known about and engaged in spiritual practices that have proven themselves to be invaluable for training our mind and body in the ways of the Kingdom. This would include a number of basic practices like solitude, reflection, memorization, meditating on a verse or phrase that we have memorized, and fasting. Unfortunately, these practices have fallen into disuse over the last few centuries, primarily because they have not been well understood or properly employed.

As stated above under *Retraining*, many Christians today equate spiritual practices with legalism or "works" of the flesh, which is an undeserved association. Most of the problems we experience with spiritual practices are not due to their basic nature, but due to the general lack of teaching and training in this important area. If we misappropriate a practice, it can certainly fall flat and cause us to be disillusioned. But learning how to participate in these practices as a means of training can alter our lives in ways we could never achieve by direct effort. Again, I will leave the actual training to other resources (see Bibliography).

In reference to our overall model of transformation, participating in restorative practices is in part the flip side of *Retraining*, which is one of the primary causes of inner change. It is important to keep both sides of this area in mind, in order to accentuate the fact that spiritual practices do not change us merely by doing them. Rather, they create a context where we can engage with God, while working something into our mental habits that we would not be able to accomplish by any direct act of our will. So even though we ourselves are the ones to initiate and persist in spiritual practices, the most significant changes that result from such practices are actually due to the presence of God and all the other resources we encounter within those practices.

It might be helpful here to spell out the differences and the relationship between *Intentionality* and *Practice*. Whereas *Intentionality* is about rearranging our life in order to become an apprentice, *Practice* refers to what we do with that space and how our very bodies are involved in the process of engaging with God. It also implies persistence. Apprenticeship is not a phase we go through, it is a life-long process of becoming more like Jesus.

In addition to classical spiritual disciplines, practice here also includes more nuanced restorative processes such as engaging in inner healing prayer and building up the contextual elements of our model which help to foster transformation. Engaging in inner healing prayer is profoundly effective in restoring our soul from old wounds and the distortions of life that arise from unresolved pain and trauma we have experienced in the past. Intentionally pursuing this kind of healing can be incredibly life changing in a relatively short time. As for building up the contexts which foster transformation, we will address that discussion in depth in the next chapter.

The apostle Paul was very keen on the value of practice and how it contributes to our overall spiritual health. We can see this very clearly in his mentoring of Timothy,.

> *Put these things into practice, devote yourself to them, so that all may see your progress. Pay close attention to yourself and to your teaching; continue in these things, for in doing this you will save both yourself and your hearers (1Tim.4:15).*

In other words, "be intentional about your practice of these things, it will change your life!" Our definition for restorative practices then runs along these lines:

> *Repeatedly pursuing and engaging in experiences that diminish our old patterns of life and support our new way of life.*

Of course, we can only skim the surface of this vast area which is covered so well in other places. Please refer to the Bibliography for further resources on what it means to participate in God's transformative processes with these resources.

## Connecting

*Fully Engaged in Authentic Relationships*

When Jesus was preparing His disciples for His nearing departure, there were a lot of important things He could have said or final thoughts He might have left with them. But more than anything else, He focused on how close their relationship would continue be, even though He would no longer be physically visible. In John 15 He used the image of a grape vine and its branches to illustrate what it would mean to *abide* in Him and how dependent upon Him they would continue to be in order to live the life He wanted them to have.

It is from this connection with God that the fruit of the Spirit emerges very naturally. Fruit does not come from trying to make fruit. It happens from abiding in the Vine. Nor is this a fancy euphemism for engaging in a lot of ministry activity. Jesus is talking about a relationship that is real and substantive, a qualitative connection from which we can draw spiritual food that changes us on the inside, producing more love, joy, peace, patience, kindness, generosity, faithfulness, gentleness and self-control (Gal.5:22-23).

Furthermore, as we have already noted, transformation is fundamentally a relational process. All of the causes for transformation come from God (sometimes through other people) not from education or circumstances or any direct effort on our part. And if all of the causes come from God and others, then learning how to engage with them so we can encounter those resources and appropriate them is absolutely essential to participating well in our formation.

That is, if I have been seriously betrayed by a friend, I need something more than my own resolve in order to work through to forgiveness. Only by engaging with God can I receive the necessary healing as well as God's view of my friend, both of which are crucial for me in order to come to terms with the betrayal. Or to state this in more general terms, I need a working relationship with God in order to receive what I need for my spiritual life.

Now when we talk about having a relationship with God, it is important to clarify what we mean by that phrase. Many Christians think they have a relationship with God simply because they "accepted Jesus as their personal savior." But while the two issues are related, they are not at all the same thing. Just as building a joyful marriage consists of a great deal more than getting married, so also connecting with God and having a relationship with Him involves a lot more than saying the sinner's prayer or reading the Bible.

Living in relationship with God means that we have some sense of His presence with us, have conversations with Him, and often feel led by the Spirit in matters of discernment. In a nutshell, this is a relationship that we actually experience, not simply talk about or imagine. And as we connect with Him in these consciously tangible ways, we also experience His truth, love, cleansing, corrective insights, and retraining of our heart and mind.

In fact, doing virtually nothing at all but resting in God's presence can be life-changing in many ways. His very presence with us can heal many of our wounds from abandonment and isolation. We can begin to feel His goodness and His heart for us in ways that calm the deepest parts of our soul. And our fear of evil begins to lose its grip as we surrender to His care.

### Connecting with Others On This Journey

There are several reasons why other members of the Body of Christ are essential in this process. For starters, most of us need to learn how to develop authentic relationships with other people before we can begin to reach out to God for a deeper relationship. It is a rare individual who first learns how to engage with God and only later is able to translate this to their human connections. While these two kinds of relationship do support each other incrementally, our starting point is most naturally with people of good character.

The reason for this is simply the ways in which our minds are wired for relationship. Giving and receiving love and good emotional gifts does not happen automatically. It is learned over time from our personal experience. As an infant, if our caregivers are kind and attentive, we will grow a capacity for joy and love and trust that will form the basis for healthy inter-dependence. That in turn gives us an experiential basis for what it means to build a relationship with God.

On the other hand, if our early experiences are hurtful and trust-breaking, then we learn to distance ourselves from others and close off our heart from whatever they might offer. We then have no experiential basis for how a relationship might actually be essential to our well-being. This makes it incredibly difficult to open ourselves to God. Trying to learn how to hear His voice or sense His presence goes against all of the internal wiring we have built over time to keep us "safe" from others.

What often breaks through this barrier is the genuine care and love of another person. Encountering authentic kindness and goodness from others can be a *corrective experience* that is powerful enough to get through our defenses and open us up to new possibilities.

As mentioned previously, this happened to me when I was thirty-four. The small group I had joined was learning how to engage with and support one another in ways that were totally foreign to my earlier experience. It was literally a shock to my system. And over time as I continued to meet with them and get to know them, I began to grow relational circuits in my mind that had never existed before. Relationships began to mean something new and different, and it changed me in ways I cannot even explain.

By the time I began learning how to engage with God a few years later, I had grown a new capacity and openness to the goodness of others who were trustworthy enough to engage with. The very meaning of *relationship* had changed and become far more rich and multi-faceted, giving me hope and confidence that God would engage with me as well. Thus it was my experiences with other people that laid a foundation for having an authentic relationship with God. And my ongoing relationships with others continue to feed my soul and to offer corrective experiences that I still need.

But equally important, we all need to give love as well as receive it. Giving away love and impacting others for good is fundamental to our need to matter and have significance in this world. This in turn is intimately connected to what it means to be fully human and a child of the King. We are never fully complete until we learn to abide in the love of God for others. The more we have to give, the more we will become like Jesus; and the more we become like Jesus, the more we will have to give.

We need each other far more than we know.

### Summary

Of all that can be said about *connecting,* one of the most important factors is that we are truly involved in the process. An authentic relationship requires our participation, whether it is with people or with God. To whatever extent we are passive, we diminish the relationship and limit how much life can come from our interaction. Even if our involvement is mostly that of an active listener or to purposely attune to the other, it matters.

Our participation will shape and form us, just as surely as it will impact the connection itself. And since *relationship* is so central to what it means to be human, interacting with God and others in life-giving ways is as important to our well-being as breathing and eating. If we skip over this in favor of a more "private" spiritual life, we will miss the very heart of God.

## Problems with Participation

At the beginning of the chapter we outlined the single greatest obstacle to participation, which is the current climate of performance-driven ideas about the spiritual life. But there are a few other issues that also get in the way of participating well with God for transformation.

## Confusing Spiritual Growth with Ministry

One of the more predictable results of the dominant performance-oriented approach to spiritual development is the tendency to confuse maturity with ministry and other religious activity. People are often told that if they want to continue to grow, they have to get involved in some church ministry. Or they are shown diagrams of how they are expected to move through the church training programs until they become leaders who try to get still others to go through the same process.

Now do not misunderstand. Learning more about the Bible and how to minister to one another is a great thing. Some organizations would do well to consider more such training. But sometimes keeping the programs going becomes a goal in itself, along with an assumption that spiritual growth will be a natural byproduct of all the activity. However, research has shown that Christian education and church involvement do very little to transform character.[13] Being involved in ministry is neither a sign of having achieved some level of maturity nor a very good catalyst for developing maturity, especially when the underlying assumptions are that growth comes from doing more.

On the other hand, ministry involvement can be a wonderful way to expose our defects and discover our limitations. It can be a great context for engaging with God for more of what we are missing and for healing whatever triggers show up as we attempt to minister. Paul made the interesting observation that no one is sufficient for ministry in any case (2Cor.2:16), which ought to drive us toward further dependency on God and make us less reliant on willpower or our own abilities in order to be truly helpful to others.

God always intends to minister to the minister, as well as those to whom the ministry is directed. When we forget that and believe the Church is

---

13 See the *Reveal* study done by Willow Creek Community Church.

divided up into those who provide ministry and those who receive it, we will miss the point and confuse effort with outcome.

### Stopping Part Way

Those who are familiar with the twelve-step movement may have noticed how dangerous it is to for a person to start their recovery and then to stop it and quit "working the program." Whether it is because such individuals believe they have achieved all they needed to or because they just get tired, the result is generally the same. They get stuck in their personal growth and everyone around them is impacted negatively by whatever unresolved issues still affect the unhealed person.

A similar problem is very common among Christians today who may have begun their spiritual journey in a blaze of glory, but over time slowed down or completely stopped their growth process. Whether they believe that most of their resolvable issues have been addressed, or if they have come to believe not much progress is really possible in this life, the unhealed and unrestored aspects will continue to impact everyone around them, as well as hinder their own life.

One of the most common symptoms of this problem can be seen when someone says or thinks to themselves, "I already know most of what I need to know, I just need to apply it." While it may be true that we know more than we have incorporated into our life, believing that I do not have much to learn truly assumes way too much. God's ways are so much higher than our ways, we will never exhaust what He wants to teach us about living in the Kingdom.

Sometimes this slowdown in growth is even expected and fostered by the larger group, which may teach that transformation is relatively rare, or that growth is roughly the same thing as training for ministry, or that it is some phase we go through before becoming "productive" members of the church.

All of these viewpoints, whether personal or corporate, will undermine the development and character transformation that is possible in Christ.

## Summary

Learning to participate well with God is a lifelong process. There is no ending point. Being intentional means continuously refocusing our eyes and ears, as well as our efforts. Becoming more receptive to what God wants to do in us is a never-ending journey. Developing relationships that are life-giving can take years to nurture and maintain. Identifying and engaging in restorative practices will foster our growth for as long as we live.

God has provided us with amazing resources for transformation. And when we learn how to participate with Him and others in order to allow those resources to change us, we become different from the inside out, more and more formed into the image of Christ.

Taking on the character of Jesus is our first and most important calling. Because only then will we truly be witnesses to what God can do in this world. And only then will we be able to participate in the work that God has prepared for each of us to do.

# Chapter 4
# A Supporting Context

At this point we now have an understanding of the primary means by which transformation happens at all, as well as a broad perspective about how we are involved in the process in order for those means to impact on our soul. What now remains is to grasp the significance of the context in which all of this takes place. Because like everything else we experience, our context helps to shape who we are. And more than that, our context can actually determine whether we have access to the means of change at all or whether we will be capable of participating in ways that matter.

While a complete list of relevant factors would be quite long, most of them can be grouped quite naturally into just a few categories. For our purposes here, we will cover what appear to be the four most important areas of concern which can make or break most of what we have discussed so far. These are:

- A Life-Giving Community
- Human Maturity
- Formationally Sound Theology
- The Isaiah 61 Ministry of God

All four of these arenas are absolutely essential. Without them there is very little possibility that we will have access to the work of transformation, or that whatever transformative experiences we do have will survive the ravages of day-to-day life in our broken world.

On the other hand, to whatever extent these contextual elements are in place, they will foster both the accessibility of the direct causes we need and enhance our ability to participate well with God and others so that we can internalize these resources and become more of who God intended us to be.

## Life Giving Community

During the last few decades, a great deal has been said about community and the lack of it in modern society. We are fundamentally relational beings, and we need each other far more than we know. Unfortunately, we have all internalized a belief in individualism that has almost as much power in our life as Newtonian physics. For most of us, all of our default assumptions about time and life and even our connections to others are heavily filtered through an exaggerated lens of the autonomous self. No matter how much we might believe objectively that community is important, relatively few of us have ever tried to arrange our lives around it.

Given that there are also various types of community, we need to be more specific about what kind of relational fabric supports transformation on an ongoing basis. For those familiar with the Life Model,[14] that is the kind of relational model we have in mind here. Some of the values that are held dear in this environment include:

- People are meant to pursue life-long restoration and development. This is about process, not arrival.
- Joy and Love are foundational to all the relationships, rather than fear or competition or some other stressful dynamic.
- Love is given freely; it does not have to be earned.
- Giving and receiving goodness is the normal way of interacting.
- Those upstream in any given area help those who are downstream from them.
- It ought to be safe to be weak and even safe to fail.

---

14 See the *Regarding Community* section in the Bibliography

Hopefully, most of us would want to live in this kind of community, at least in our better moments of clarity. What stops us is the sheer disbelief that any such arrangement would be possible; or the conviction that if someone ever did get such a community going it would not last very long.

But while we may not know of any perfect community that we could go join, we can certainly create elements of this relational atmosphere among friends who are like-minded and who want a better way of life. Going back to the discussion about intentionality, creating life-giving connections is largely a matter of deciding that it matters enough to arrange our lives to make a space for our relationships. And of course that also means seeking out whatever healing we need in order to foster, build and sustain those connections.

There are several reasons why I believe this kind of community is part of the necessary context for ongoing transformation. For starters, life is all about relationship. We were not designed to live in a vacuum or merely for our own personal benefit. Nor do we pursue transformation just so we can be more integrated on the inside. Our goal is to be able to relate to God and others in the spirit of joy and shalom, and to be part of what God is doing in the world to create a genuinely good Kingdom family.

Secondly, relationships are entirely dependent upon a complex suite of emotionally-laden, interactive, *acquired relational competencies*. A major part of healthy human development requires that we learn how to relate to others in an emotionally intelligent and competent manner. These "skills" are learned by interacting with and watching others who already possess them. That is how we internalize their meaning and value.

For example, one of the more challenging relational problems we face is how to repair a relationship after some kind of rupture has taken place. If one person hurts another, either intentionally or not, a lot of spiritual and emotional work may be required in order to reconcile, forgive, and restore trust to that relationship. And we have all experienced times where this process is beyond our ability. Sometimes with time and considerable effort we are able to fully restore the relationship, and other times the obstacles are just too great for either one or both parties involved.

The point here is that relational maturity is not innate, but a broad set of competencies we may acquire over a lifetime. Again, in order to learn these skills we need others with whom we can relate in healthy, life-giving ways. There is no other way to learn them.

Third, other people are a major source for corrective experiences that can change our life. If our first family was severely deficient in some way, we were probably unable to grow up as God intended, and instead may have internalized a number of coping systems which are not healthy for us. Given the incredible needs of small children, even good families can leave lasting scars on children which need to be attended to in later life. This is why daily encounters with others who have different resources than we have can actually become life-changing corrective experiences.

Fourth, the stronger our relational capacities, the better our relationship with God will be. As we continue to develop relational competencies, we can go deeper with God, build stronger bonds with Him, and even work better with Him as He renews our mind and heals our wounds.

Of course this also works in a circular manner. As our relationship with God grows deeper, we are more able to relate to others, and even more able to grow our relational competencies.

Finally, it needs to be said again that life is all about relationship. Life is not about winning competitions, accumulating the most toys, becoming famous, or having the most followers on Twitter. A person who has a good life is one who is loved well, and who loves others well and cares about their well-being. More than anything else, this is why we need a context of life-giving community in order to become the people God created us to be.

## Basic Human Development

As hinted above, a life-giving community is made up of healthy, well-developed individuals. Or more accurately, a strong symbiotic relationship exists between human development and community health. Each one is predicated on the other and supports the other.

As is the case with community, the process of human development has been studied extensively over the last several decades. However, many of these models tend to view the human person in very autonomous terms, with other people being involved only on the periphery.[15] Once we grasp how fundamental relationships are to human development, that kind of lens is no longer sufficient.

This is where the Life Model really shines. According to this model, the very definition of maturity is *the ability to manage increasingly complex relationships with joy and competence*. In other words, human development is defined almost entirely in *relational* terms. For example, an infant needs to learn how to trust and interact with their primary care-givers; a child learns to relate to other children; adults need to develop a group identity and develop a sense of "us"; parents must learn to relate sacrificially to their own children, and elders must learn how to give themselves for the good of the larger community, and do so joyfully. Each step in maturity is defined in terms of how our relationships grow and become more complex.

Furthermore, these "stages" of maturity are highly inter-dependent and interactive, such that a person in one stage grows by interacting with people who are at other levels of maturity. The most obvious of these is the parent-infant or parent-child interaction, in which both persons are changed by the relationship and both are agents for change within the relationship. But this need to interact with people of different maturity levels applies to everyone.

---

15 Alfred Adler was a notable exception to this emphasis on the individual.

Since a full exploration of human maturity is beyond the scope of this book, the reader is referred to the Bibliography for those resources. What we want to emphasize here is that just as personal growth and relationships are deeply intertwined and actually inseparable, there also exists in similar fashion a symbiotic relationship between human development and spiritual development.

For example, one of the basic relational competencies that an infant needs to learn is *how to quiet* their mind and emotions though interacting with another person and receiving what they have to offer by way of comfort, empathy, and so on. If we do not learn how to do this, then our inability to quiet can become a barrier to engaging with God, who usually speaks to us in subtle ways which are easily overwhelmed by noise in our mind. So to whatever extent we can learn to quiet with others, we will be better able to quiet in the presence of God and discern His promptings.

Conversely, the better we are able to engage with God, the more at peace we will be in our soul and the easier it will be to return to quiet after we have been upset by something. Thus our acquired human ability helps us to engage with God and our relationship with God makes our human task more achievable. Or to put this another way, proper human development provides a wonderful context for spiritual growth and transformation, and as we become more like Jesus, we are able to build a stronger context.

Another important acquired relational competency is our *capacity* to handle distressful emotions like shame or anger and at the same time stay emotionally present and relationally connected to those around us. Being able to feel shame and stay relational at the same time in the presence of another person whom we have hurt can be an important part of offering an authentic apology. But if we are able to tolerate very little shame or none at all (which is extremely common) then staying connected long enough to repair ruptures will be nearly impossible. We need to be able to regulate our pain well enough to stay connected to others in healthy ways.

Now consider the task of engaging with God in a manner similar to what we see in Psalm 139. "Search me O God and know my heart ... see if there is anything evil or hurtful in there that needs to change." If we have developed the human capacity to handle shame and restoration at the same time, then we are more likely to feel safe enough to expose all our dirt in the presence of God. And the more we learn to be transparent before God with all our shame, the safer we will feel while engaging with others when we are feeling shame, thereby growing our capacity for emotional distress. Again we see an interactive relationship between human development and spiritual growth.

The list of ways in which this works is literally as long as the number of human relational and emotional abilities. Human maturity aids our spiritual development, and spiritual growth enables more human maturity. Once we get the nature of this, it should become obvious that this would be how God intended for us to grow up. After all, many of the fruits of the Spirit are really about improving our emotional life and our loving relationships with others: love, joy, gentleness, self-control, and so on.

We would expect *immaturity*, humanly speaking, to be quite a barrier to spiritual development and transformative experience. Similarly, we should anticipate that good human development provides a necessary context for the ongoing process of character transformation.

## Formationally Sound Theology

Not only do we need a coherent theology of transformation, we also need a larger context of practical theology that is supportive and consistent with this entire theme. The truth is that during the last two hundred years or so, most seminaries have been extremely weak in this area, and have not trained pastors and teachers with the tools to address this problem. Consequently, commonly accepted understandings of very basic doctrines among leaders and laypersons alike are often diametrically opposed to any workable approach to spiritual growth and development. Yet relatively few Christians are aware of how these commonly accepted theologies actually derail their efforts to grow spiritually, or how prevalent they really are.

For many, statements like this immediately raise serious concerns. What doctrines are you talking about? What are you challenging here? How can such distortions be as common as you say? These are good questions, and they will be addressed shortly. But to be honest, most people find theological discussions to be far too boring to even consider thinking about such things. Which of course is what makes it easy for distorted ideas to persist and flourish. But unless we think seriously about the implications of what we believe, it is easy to accept whatever we hear as long as it sounds plausible enough. And for a variety of reasons, the prevailing ideas about spiritual growth and development have been terribly distorted for several generations. Yet until fairly recently they have been largely unchallenged.

So what are these distorted beliefs that can be heard every Sunday in church? We have already named a few, but at this point we want to be completely clear about what we are referring to. For starters, consider for a moment the following observation along with its serious implications.

David Benner says he often asks Christians a simple question: "Imagine God thinking about you. What do you assume God feels when you come to mind?" Interestingly, one of the most common responses he hears is *disappointment*.[16] Now there could be a number of reasons for this reaction. Some, no doubt, feel as if they have been neglecting their spiritual life or pursuing things they know are not good for them. They are disappointed in themselves, so they assume God is, too. But I would argue that this negative perception of God's opinion is really symptomatic of two larger problems.

First, given that relatively few Christian organizations know how to help people participate well in their own spiritual formation, many people really

16 David Benner, *Surrender to Love*, p.15

do suffer from a lack of growth and are understandably disappointed in their progress. But the truth is that if God is disappointed at all, it is probably with the Christian community at large for not being honest about our overall spiritual anemia or taking it seriously enough to look for help.

Second, much of the sense of God's disapproval which people struggle with is rooted in what can only be described as distorted images of who God is and how He wants to be involved in our lives. If we see God primarily as an observing judge who simply watches and condemns what is bad, then we might have reason to fear His gaze. We might even hope that God does not think about us too often. And if such distorted images of God are that common, what does that say about the practical theology that is being passed around, either explicitly or implicitly?

What we believe about things matters a great deal, because our beliefs drive all of our strategies for moving forward, or in many cases, prevent the creation of any real strategy. Frankly, there is enough *anti-tranformational theology* circulating around the Christian world to warrant an entire volume to address them adequately. But a short preview is certainly called for here. Hopefully this will be sufficient to identify the serious nature of the problems we face.

## A God Who Speaks

As a teenager, my church taught me that God stopped talking at the end of the first century and gave us the Bible as His last word and our only source of God's revelation to us. Anyone who claimed to "hear" from God had to be deceived or delusional (or both).

This limits prayer down to a one-way conversation in which I express my thoughts and desires to God, but I am left with almost no idea what God's thoughts are on any given personal issue that I am praying about. If I want to know God's will in some area, I am supposed to rely on the following three guidelines: the Bible, circumstances, and friends.

But quite honestly, this is not the kind of help that it claims to be. If I am wondering whether to quit my job in order to become a missionary, the Bible ambiguously tells me to "remain where you are" (1Cor.7:24) and "leave all" (Mt.4:20). Circumstances are no help either. If I get offered a new job with a raise, is this God's gift and His way of telling me to stay in the corporate world, or is Satan tempting me with something to keep me from going into missions? Furthermore, my friends are all having the same problems with the Bible and circumstances that I am, so their wisdom is not much better than mine. How then am I supposed to figure out God's will from three sources that raise more questions than answers? Using this approach, I am not much better off than a non-Christian in evaluating circumstances or choosing a relevant text or considering the opinions of my friends. Nothing about this process helps me know what God might want me to know, or to know whether He even cares what I decide to do.

The only honest conclusion that can be drawn from this is that if we cannot hear from the Holy Spirit, then we are actually left to our own wits about how to proceed in life. And that flies in the face of all the New Testament teaching about being led by God. Yet this kind of teaching goes on all the time as though it makes perfect sense and could actually be done with some level of assurance that we are following God's will.

And this is just the tip of the iceberg. So much more could be said about the problems created by the belief that God has fallen silent. The worst part is the fact that it is nearly impossible to have a working relationship with a God who does not speak. Which is why the phrase "relationship with God" has been altered over time to mean little more than "being a Christian." The most important thing missing in our relationship with God is *relationship.*

Dismissing the voice of God like this is just one of many ways that well-meaning theologians have nailed shut the door to the Kingdom. Context matters.

## Christian Identity

While attending seminary I read an article about an ongoing debate a certain denomination was having in regard to why Christians still sin. On the one side was the idea that Christians are fundamentally saints, but sin because they are still in need of renewal by the Holy Spirit. At the other end of the spectrum were those who said that if we were saints we would not sin, and so the reason Christians sin is because we are basically still sinners. We have received a pardon and will go to heaven and be transformed when we die, but in the mean time not much can be expected to change.

What disturbed me about this article was the fact that any serious theologian could espouse such a negative theory of Christian identity, such that very little changes at conversion and we are all still sinners. It seems to me you would have to gut much of the New Testament to come up with a view of the Christian life so devoid of victory or any ability to eradicate sin. This to me sounds like an attempt to explain why spiritual growth is so elusive for so many Christians, rather than a serious exploration of Christian identity. Adopting such a view totally robs us of any hope of real change. Dallas Willard fittingly referred to this as "miserable sinner" Christianity.

Another doctrine of Christian identity today which is wide-spread but just as debilitating in its impact on Christian formation is the *two-nature theory*. In this view, Christians retain the "old nature" they were born with and God gives them a "new nature" that moves in alongside the old one. Our challenge then is to learn how to give the new nature more say in our daily walk, and reduce the influence of the old nature. The reason we still sin is because we have not fully repressed the old nature.

Now at first glance, this gives us some reason to hope for victory. If only we could train our will to do what is right, we can become a better person. However, a closer look at this theory will show how flawed it truly is.

First of all, how is one supposed to arbitrate between these two natures? Do we have a *third* nature that makes choices between a bad nature and a good one? Is our will really independent of our two most basic natures?

And if our old nature is depraved and incapable of change and our new nature is perfect and does not need change, how do we change? Is the entire process of sanctification merely about training our will to make better choices? Small wonder so much of the Church has been captivated by a performance-driven approach to spiritual development! This distorted sense of Christian identity leaves little room for any other approach.

In either of the above theories, the miserable sinner identity or the two-nature identity, it is almost impossible to formulate a coherent theology of sanctification, because neither one offers any hope for eradicating sin, nor is there anything in the person which is capable of transformation. The end result is a bankrupt approach to spiritual growth that relies almost entirely on willpower and the belief that if you try really hard to do the right things, God will help you.

If we are to have any true understanding of Christian identity, it must be drawn from all of the New Testament. But Paul summarizes it quite well in Colossians 3:9-10.

> *You have put off the old nature and put on a new nature that is being renewed after the knowledge of the one who created you. (PAR)*

According to Paul, our new nature is *not* perfect, it is in the process of being renewed. That is why we still sin. But renewal is real. This gives us a place to begin envisioning a life of transformation!

Yes, we still have to deal with the conflict that exists between flesh and spirit (Gal.5:17), but that is not at all the same thing as a conflict between the old nature and new nature (which never exist at the same time in the same person). These are two very different discussions.

The point here is that distorted images of Christian identity can destroy any hope of transformation. And when theology leads us away from any hope of real change, then the theology has to be wrong, no matter how well intentioned. Context matters.

### The Good News

Another major contribution to the anemia of modern Christianity has to do with the way the gospel itself is presented. More often than not, the good news is reduced to a way of securing our eternal destiny. "Would you like to know for sure you will go to heaven when you die?"

The problem here is that this message leaves out the most important part. "Would you like to turn your life over to God and learn from Jesus how to live your life?" That would be a lot more in line with Jesus' invitation, "Come and follow me."

When the gospel is presented as if it had little to do with relationship or commitment, but merely to stamp our visa for the afterlife, it is gutted of its most significant elements. Willard called this "a truncated gospel." Far more important than being saved from hell, we need to be saved from ourselves and from sin and what it has done to our soul. Our salvation from hell is actually a secondary result of being cleansed and reborn into the family of God, not the other way around.

Anyone who accepts this empty invitation to heaven is then in the curious position of needing *additional* incentives and invitations in order to agree to a life of discipleship and spiritual growth. It is not much of a leap then to arrive at a practical theology that tells us God's part was to provide eternal life, and our part is to follow His commands. So once again we are back to trying hard to measure up to God's standards rather than learning how to participate in transformation. In this way, the truncated gospel tends to hide from us the fundamental nature of spiritual development.

The gospel is really good news about the present availability of the Kingdom of God! Transformation is possible. We can be cleansed and live a more abundant life than we ever imagined. Context matters.

### Conclusion

We could go on with an entire book about commonly accepted practical theologies that are anti-transformational in nature. The modern Christian world has been overrun by them. But ideas have consequences. And when our practical ideas about how life works in the Kingdom are distorted, we lose something important and spend our energy in pursuit of things that do not satisfy (Isa.55:1-3).

Transformation is either fostered or hindered by what we believe. Our theological context is vital to our hope for change. That is why it is so important to clarify our practical theology and to correct the errors that threaten our spiritual vitality. May we have the courage to admit where we have been mistaken and do the work of reclaiming our rightful inheritance and the gifts God has for us.

## Isaiah 61 Ministry of God

With all that has been said already, transformation would not be possible at all without God in us, working with us and for us to restore our heart and mind, changing us from the inside out to become more and more like Jesus. Although this is obviously an underlying assumption behind any reasonable theory of transformation, there are several reasons why it is important to point this out explicitly.

First, whenever we are detailing practical steps designed to help people in their spiritual journey, there is always a tendency on the part of many to focus on the steps themselves in ways that distort the process. In our current performance-oriented religious climate, this is particularly problematic, because nearly everything said about the spiritual life is interpreted by the reader or listener as part of a "how-to" lesson, even before it is given any serious consideration.

I would like to suggest that it would be far more accurate to view this model as a description of "who-with" or "how-with-God," rather than "how-to." By that I mean *everything about transformation needs to be viewed within a relational context*. This is all about how we are to be engaged with God as His child and apprentice, in order to participate with both what He is doing in us and what He is doing in the world with us.

God really is here, working to overcome evil with good. That includes the evil in us as well as the evil in our immediate sphere of influence. It is no good to believe that when Jesus ascended back to His Father we were left on our own to "do our best" until He returned. Ideas like this effectively strip the present Kingdom of its power to restore and heal our broken lives, and remove any hope of experiencing the reality of Isaiah 61 in our daily existence.

The truth is, when Jesus returned to His Father, He went from the seen world to the unseen world where He could be at work in every place at once, rather than be limited to one place at a time. He has not gone far, far away, reachable only by praying across a chasm in the hope that He will hear us. He is both present with us and actively at work in those who seek Him and participate with Him for all that He desires to do in their life.

Our take-away from all this is that we must learn how to train the eyes of our heart to see the "unseen real" around us, which Tozer spoke of so extensively (and more recently Leanne Payne). For too long the Christian world has focused on behavior and boundary markers to tell us right from wrong, and who is in and who is out. To do so is to "set our eyes on things of this world" (Col.3:2) rather than the unseen realities which really matter. As a result, many have so lowered their expectations of Kingdom Life as to rob it almost entirely of its power to change lives. Learning to see with our heart what cannot be seen with our eyes is crucial to changing who we are.

Lastly, we must forever dismiss this terrible idea that "it is up to us" to live out the Christian life. One of the many distorted perceptions of the New Covenant that I grew up with was the idea that "salvation is something God does out of His love for us, and the Christian life is what we do for God out of our love for Him." And a close corollary to that was the belief that God gave us the Bible so we could figure out the lessons learned by the people there and then try to apply those lessons to our own life. If anything, the Bible demonstrates conclusively that we cannot live well apart from an authentic interactive relationship with God. Yet one would think such a relationship is impossible or a New Age heresy, based on the religion of self-effort most of us have been sold.

More recently I heard another version of this mistaken approach to life which taught that God takes care of the negatives in our life, such as our sin and our wounds, but it is up to us to achieve all the positive movement in our character formation and spiritual development. The implications of such teaching is staggering, and the harm it leaves in its wake is incalculable. As stated earlier, while the human process of emotional and relational development is essential to long-term transformation, thinking we can reach some point in our development where the rest is up to us is about as foolish and destructive to the body of Christ as it can be.

God's work to restore and redeem what is broken is only the beginning of life with Him. Growing up into the character of Christ is a life-long process (or perhaps even longer!) that also requires the work of God. We are no more capable of taking on the nature of Jesus than we are capable of eradicating the sin in our life. These all need the power of God as envisioned in Isaiah 61 and elsewhere.

Learning to see with the eyes of our heart and to engage continuously with God for His work in us is at the very core of transformation. May we look for Him with all our heart, soul, mind and strength, and learn to live in the realities of the unseen world all around us.

## Summary

If we are to have any hope of transformation becoming common-place among Christians, we will need a supporting context of emotional and relational maturity, healthy community, formationally sound theology, and an ongoing experience of Isaiah's vision. To foster these elements is to foster transformation. To miss any one of these areas is to impair our access to the changes in character which all true Christians desire. As Peter reminds us,

> *"His divine power has given us everything needed for life and godliness, through the knowledge of him who called us by his own glory and goodness. Thus he has given us, through these things, his precious and very great promises, so that through them you may escape from the corruption that is in the world because of lust, and may become participants of the divine nature (2Pet.1:3-4).*

God has provided everything we need for life and godliness, if only we will learn how to pursue these gifts as well as God Himself. Building the context to support this pursuit is essential to our well-being. May God give us eyes to see and ears to hear, what His Spirit has for us all.

# Chapter 5
# Mistaken Ideas of Transformation

Wherever the issues of Christian living and discipleship are taken seriously, two topics in particular tend to dominate the discussion, almost to the exclusion of anything else. They are the twin areas of *repentance* and *obedience*. Because of their inherent connection to our focus on authentic discipleship, it would not be possible to cover the topic of transformation without addressing these issues.

In many Christian circles, these processes are considered absolutely foundational to any approach to spiritual growth and development. Sin is a reality in our life, and thus we need to understand and practice repentance. And following Jesus means doing what He says to do, making obedience absolutely necessary.

In essence, these are true enough. But the problem is that these two areas have been absorbed over time into the ever-present pervasive climate of performance-driven Christianity. Repentance and obedience as taught today have much more in common with behavior modification than they do with true discipleship. The impact of such distorted approaches to repentance and obedience has been nothing short of devastating. In fact, both of these issues have been redefined and modified so much that they now actually reinforce our culture of religious performance.

For reasons which will become obvious, we need to stop and examine repentance and obedience in order to revision both of them from a formational perspective. In doing so, we will truly reinforce the value of both, as well as demonstrate how they are fully represented in our model of transformation.

## True Repentance

*Engaging with God for a Change of Heart*

For starters, let me say categorically that the model of transformation presented in this work is, in its entirety, all about repentance! Hopefully, this will become clear as we proceed. But the point is that just because the word "repentance" was not used much in the previous chapters does not mean that it has been forgotten or ignored.

In the New Covenant sense of the word, to repent means that our eyes have been opened to what is real and true about our self, we recognize how far we have fallen short of God's design for us – both intentionally and unintentionally, and as a result we come to God and surrender to whatever He wants to do in us for restoration and growth.

David himself had this understanding of repentance when he wrote Psalm 51. Nowhere in this psalm does he promise to try hard to be a better person. There is no hint at all of making a new resolution or exercising his will to overcome his sin. Instead, he casts himself fully on God and asks Him to give him a new heart that would never conceive of such evil. He is asking God to do for him what he could never do for himself. Repentance for David had nothing whatever to do with resolving to do the right things. It had much more to do with understanding that his "resolver" was the cause of the problem in the first place. He needed more than a different resolution. He needed a new heart. He needed God to do something way beyond what He could do by his own will.

Unfortunately, this was not at all how I was taught repentance in my early years as a Christian. Repentance was something shameful, awful, and a thing to be avoided if at all possible. It meant I had to beat myself up, feel as badly as I possibly could about who I was and what I had done, and swear on my life never to do those things again, begging God for forgiveness and hoping to be contrite enough to get Him to forgive me.

But we do not see any of that here in this psalm, even though it has become the quintessential prayer of repentance. Instead, David brings his broken soul to God and asks Him to create a new heart to replace the one that got so distorted he didn't even know how he was involved in his own worst moment. "God, You need to do something in me I cannot do myself!" That's a far cry from the kinds of resolutions we try to make in the name of repentance.

David's approach is much more representative of true repentance. In essence he says, "My God has a good heart. I will go to Him with my sin. For He alone knows how to cleanse me and heal me, so I can be close to Him again."

Or to put this all another way, "I need to be transformed because I do not want to be the kind of person who would do those things. I want to be different in ways I cannot accomplish by my own direct effort." This is in fact what our model of transformation actually portrays. That is why we can say the model is all about repentance, and why trying to add the prevailing distorted concept of repentance to this model would only distort it. What most of us were taught about repentance is in truth *anti-transformational* in nature. Trying to feel bad enough or try hard enough to bring about change is totally antithetical to God's way of renewing our heart. The best we can do with our will is to turn our focus toward God for the cleansing of the old and the imparting of the new that we need.

Viewed in this way, repentance is no longer a dreaded experience of shame and self-hate. It is instead an act of surrender to God's offer to rescue us from our own devices. This results in an actual experience of God's love and grace at work in us to transform our heart and mind to be more like Him. The possibility that we could be different than we are right now is our greatest hope (1Jn.3). And to encounter God time and again for this kind of change is not only a privilege, but something to be desired more than life itself.

## True Obedience

*Becoming a Fully Committed Apprentice of Jesus*

The other area that usually comes up when discussing spiritual growth and development is that of obedience. We are told over and over that in order to be a good Christian and in order to grow spiritually, we must try to be obedient to what Jesus said to do.

Once again, we would agree that obedience is absolutely essential. But how obedience is understood in our performance-driven religious context is not at all what Jesus meant by the term. That is where the problem lies. Obedience as it is taught in most Christian circles today means using our raw willpower to try hard to do what Jesus said, and to not do what He said to avoid. However, as should be clear by now, that kind of willful "obedience" will not transform our heart and mind.

In fact we end up with the exact opposite result. Because if our only reason for doing something or not doing something is because we are trying to be obedient, what does that say about our heart and mind? The very fact that we have to try hard to override something else inside us should throw up red flags all over the place – that something is wrong inside, something we are trying to repress rather than transform!

Obedience under the New Covenant was never meant to be the act of conforming to an external standard of behavior. That is much closer to what obedience meant under the Old Covenant. Moreover, it is an approach which Paul said never worked! Why so much of the Christian world insists on employing an Old Covenant process is truly bewildering. Its utter failure to produce real change ought to be obvious to anyone who is willing to look at the evidence.

Of course most of this teaching also claims that since we have the Holy Spirit we can do a better job than the Israelites did under the law. The basic idea here is that the Holy Spirit gives us the strength to do what they could not do. And while this may sound plausible, it simply does not hold up under examination. This is neither the Holy Spirit's primary role in our life, nor is it very accurate in terms of the differences between the two covenants.

As long as we treat Jesus' commands like a new and improved version of the law, a set of principles that we are supposed to live up to, it does no good to imagine that we can do so because of the Holy Spirit's presence. God is not really very interested in helping us comply with an external standard, and that is not the Holy Spirit's job.

Rather than trying to live up to laws written on stone or principles written in the New Testament, God has made it abundantly clear that He intends to transform us from the inside out, by writing His laws on our heart and mind. To put it another way, our hope for change comes from God's intention to literally change how we think and respond, to do a work in us that results in our actually internalizing His goodness, not merely attempting to imitate it or comply with it. The difference between the two covenants in this matter is like night and day.

This is why Jesus talked so much about the difference between a good tree and a defective one, about cleaning the inside of the cup so the outside could become clean as well. This is also why Paul argued so strongly against legalism in the early church and its potential to rob Christians of the life God intended for them. Our goal is not to try to act more like Jesus, but to actually become more like Jesus.

That changes everything we thought we knew about obedience, because it can no longer be about trying hard to do the right things. Obedience to Jesus is instead about becoming His apprentices and learning from Him how to become more of who He designed us to be. Being a disciple of a rabbi was never about trying to *mimic* the teacher. Students of a rabbi were in training to *become* like their teacher in every way possible: in outlook, in character, and in their very nature. Jesus referred to this process when He said, "Everyone, after he has been fully trained, will be like his teacher" (Lk.6:40 NASB). That is the point.

True obedience, then, is about submitting to our training, which is a multifaceted relational process involving intentionality, receptivity, and practice, the very things we show in this model. And since obedience to a beloved mentor bears no resemblance at all to the kind of obedience demanded by a drill instructor, we can only understand what obedience means by examining the context to which it applies. And the context of apprenticeship to Jesus is an incredible relationship that He wants to have with us so that He can renew us from the inside out.

## Summary

Repentance and obedience are certainly two very important over-arching themes interwoven though Scripture. But without a clear understanding of what is meant by these terms, it is very easy to fall into the highly reductionistic view of them which has dominated much of the Christian world for a long time. Consequently, it is incumbent upon us to make sure we separate both obedience and repentance from any distorted theology that is rooted in self-effort.

Once we bring these concepts into alignment with a larger view that is consistent with transformation, we can then begin to understand them as they were intended. Both areas help to shed light on what it means to participate well with God for change, but only when they are seen within that larger framework of transformation.

My prayer is that we will redeem both of these terms from their currently abused status, and restore the practices of true repentance and true obedience back into the fabric of our training and discipleship efforts.

# Chapter 6
# Why It Matters

Having described a robust model of transformation, including what causes it, what fosters it, and how we are involved, a number of questions emerge that need to be addressed. Why do we need a model anyway? What purpose does it serve? Is this just a theoretical discussion for theologians to argue about, or does it have some practical value for the average layperson?

The short answer to these questions is this: *Whatever beliefs we have about transformation effect all of us a great deal.* Ideas have consequences. If our practical theology of spiritual development teaches us that our primary task is try our best to measure up to some ideal standard of morality or behavior, then we will likely dismiss transformation as an unnecessary or out-of-reach visionary ideal, and miss the abundant life, about which the New Testament has so much to say. And if our theology has little to say at all about transformation, it is unlikely that we will see much of it in our Christian organizations.

Casting a vision for what is possible is absolutely crucial to the future of the Christian Church. Spiritual anemia permeates much of the Christian world precisely because it is now commonly assumed that transformation is a relatively rare, mysterious phenomena, and the best we can hope for is to develop a program of spiritual behavior modification that elevates willpower far above its rightful place.

Unless Christian leaders believe that transformation is both possible and highly accessible, they will not be able to train their people in how to engage with God for change, and will instead find themselves defaulting to the dominant performance-driven approach to spiritual development. No other options really exist. And for those leaders who do believe transformation ought to be more common and yet are not quite sure how to foster it, they actually run the risk of holding out a hope for their people that never really comes to fruition. Over time that kind of false hope can cause people to become disillusioned and give up on the abundant life altogether.

If we do not know where we need to go, then it is highly unlikely that we will ever get somewhere worthwhile. That is why we need a refresher in the theology of transformation. Because once we grasp how wide and how high the possibilities are, and once we taste of the wonders of being renewed by the hand of God, everything else about the Christian life changes!

## Love From a Pure Heart

> *The aim of our instruction and training is this: love from a pure heart (1Tim.1:5 PAR).*
>
> *Live in Love (Eph.5:2)*

The more we are transformed into the image of Christ and the more we see life through the eyes of heaven, the more we will discover who God created us to be and how God intended for us to live.

But transformation is not just about our inner life and what God can do in us. Becoming more like Jesus also changes how we see those around us and how we relate to them and interact with them. This is in fact why God goes to all the trouble of transforming us in the first place. He is a God of love. And what He wants for His children more than anything is for them to reflect His character and His love.

A great many books have been written about agape love and what it looks like when it is fleshed out in everyday life, and we will not try to duplicate any of that here. The one point that needs to be stated for the sake of clarity is that love comes from a pure heart, not from a strong will.

Many have described Christian love in various ways, such as "love is a choice" or that we are "commanded to love" and for those reasons we must do whatever we can to act in loving ways whether we want to or not. And in the absence of any genuine change of heart, doing something good for another person by choice alone is certainly preferable to doing nothing at all or being self-centered.

But what if we extended ourselves for the good of another person simply because we actually preferred doing so? What if our heart became so full of love that we truly desired what was good for others enough to do something about it? What if love came out of a transformed heart rather than from grit and strong determination? Would that not be more like the way God loves?

Whatever element of choice there might be in a genuine loving act, if we try to reduce love to little more than an act of the will to "do the right thing," then we are probably not showing the love of God at all! It might be good. It might even feel loving to whoever is on the receiving end. But it is definitely something other than the kind of love God wants us to have in our heart to give away. It is something other than the kind of love God has for us.

God is love (1Jn.4:8). It is in His very nature to love. If we ever want to love the way God loves, then we need to become more like Him in the very depths of our being. And that will only come about by change that we are not capable of on our own.

### More Than Self Improvement

Of course some people want to be healed and restored so they can then go about their personal ambitions unhindered by the weight of unhealed wounds of the past. They want to be changed because they are tired of being miserable and want some relief. The last thing they want to pursue is a way of life that considers the needs of others.

To be clear, a person who is overwhelmed by grief or pain or sin is probably in no position to think about how they might become a giving person. It would be like adding yet one more burden on an already overburdened heart. Generally speaking, transformation for most people is a gradual process. And only when a person begins to live in joy and peace do they discover they have something that they want others to have as well. This is actually another reason why teaching that love is an act of obedience does very little to motivate wounded people to be more loving.

But the vision of love that Paul is portraying in his letter to Timothy is incredibly important. Joy and peace are wonderful gifts from God that come with healing and growth, and we ought to relish the goodness that accompanies our restoration. Nothing in Paul's ideal is meant to detract from how important those treasures are for us. Yet we were never meant to stop there.

As we continually receive more life from Him and become more free from the wounds and sins of our past, we discover experientially what it means to be *filled to overflowing*. His abundant grace in our life makes it possible for us to pour out goodness and love to others. It is a lot like those water fountains that contain multiple pitchers arranged one above the other, where the water from each pitcher pours into the next and the next. That is how we can offer life to others.

We cannot give from an empty well. But as we become more and more alive in the Spirit, and as we are formed more and more into the person God created us to be, then at some point we begin to overflow and pour out the goodness of God to others. Otherwise, we will eventually put a wedge in our process and our spiritual life will begin to dry up.

### Being Kind to Ourselves As We Grow in Love

When looking at the big picture of where we are headed, we must take into consideration the fact that certain kinds of wounds of the heart can be the very thing that makes loving a hard thing to do. Even after a great deal of healing and spiritual growth, some Christians find themselves in a place where they truly want to be more loving and more giving, but the very thought of it makes them want to shut down and hide. The causes for these type of barriers are not easy to identify, nor do they necessarily resolve quickly in the healing process.

We must be patient with ourselves in all of this and continue our process of engaging with God for all that He has for us. There is no deadline by which time you "should" be measuring up to some sort of standard of what is a loving person. Nor is there normally a place of arrival after which you should be able to give as much as you receive. For most of us, this begins in very small ways and grows over time along with our continued restoration and growth. To love from a pure heart is our *aim*, not a heavy burden or some guilt trip.

But rest assured that love is good! Good for the one who is loving, as well as for the one who is being loved. When we give out of abundance it does not feel like an imposition or an obligation. In Christ it becomes a wonder and privilege. To be part of what God is doing in the earth is a great honor. And when we have been given more than we can receive, it is not so hard to give after all.

## How This Model of Transformation Helps Us

Perhaps the single most striking thing about this model is how visibly comprehensive transformation really is. Transformation is not just one thing, nor can it ever be reduced to one "formula for success." We have an amazing God who has given us multiple resources for recovery from our own failures, as well as from what this world has done to us and continues to do to us every day, and from those good things that have been left undone.

We have not been left with just a standard to live up to or only one kind of prayer that will help us mature. God has designed an incredible, multifaceted process to help us become more and and more like Jesus, day after day, as we learn how to participate with the good things He brings into our life. He is a rich and generous God. And He wants us to know what He has given to us, so that we can become who He intended for us to be.

But that is just the beginning.

One very important contribution made by this model is that it helps to demystify the notion that transformation of character is some sort of rare event. Rather, this is what God intends for all His children throughout their lives. Furthermore, the fact that we can define a workable path for authentic change means we have within our grasp a real alternative to the try-hard performance-driven approach which has dominated Christianity for at least the last two hundred years.

Sadly, many Christians have never even heard of another way to pursue spiritual growth. Suggesting there is another way raises a whole host of questions for which they have no answer. If we are to leave this self-effort behind, what can possibly take its place? How do we pursue the Christian life if it is not up to us to work it all out by sheer effort?

Unless Christians have a clear understanding of how this all works, they will never give up their current methods which are rooted in self-effort. Casting a meaningful vision of how transformation actually happens is an essential starting point for confidently pursuing a path that leads to more and more life.

Additionally, this model helps us discern the difference between training which is compatible with a journey of transformation and that which is not. For example, when we try to apply a lesson we learned in Sunday School and have trouble making it "stick," what do we do then? If the only answer we have is to try harder, or to take it more seriously, or to turn to some other form of self-effort, then we will find it hard to grow. But if we have some grasp of transformation, it will become obvious to us that we are missing something that can only be received from God. That in turn may lead us to a process of real change.

Or suppose someone presents a model of Christian identity that assumes bondage to sin is inescapable. With a robust theology of transformation in hand we do not have to wonder whether or not that view of Christian identity is true. It fails the test of whether or not it fosters transformation, and so we know it must be mistaken.

Most of all, what this model offers us is hope. All my life I have been around people who were truly committed and serious about their Christian life. But most of them were as confused as I was about how to actually change from the inside out. We wanted to become more Christ-like. But for the most part we all felt more like the wretched man of Romans seven: "I do what I don't want to do, and I cannot seem to do what I wish I could do" (Rom.7:15 PAR). Still we pushed on, hoping that someday we might somehow emerge from the fog and become more of who we hoped we could be.

But what if there was a way to actually change our heart and mind to be more like the heart and mind of Jesus? What if we could actually be transformed? What if we could become a good tree which produces good fruit by its very nature?

For nearly forty years, I was taught to focus on trying to produce better fruit. Do this and do that. Don't do the other thing. The problem was, no one seemed to know how the tree itself could change and become a fruit-bearing tree. *But instead of trying to make better fruit, we need to learn how to become a better tree.* Then the fruit will happen. Instead of trying hard to perform, we can pursue a path of becoming more the person God intends for us to be. Instead of trying to act like Jesus, we become more and more like Jesus on the inside.

Having a vision of how to proceed makes all the difference.

## For Leaders and Teachers

For those of us who have taught or fostered a try-hard approach to spiritual growth, however unintentionally, this may all be somewhat disconcerting. It may even feel as if a lot is at stake, including our own credibility. I know, I taught anti-transformational theology myself for several decades. And it is hard to admit when we are wrong about things that are so important and impact so many people.

But if we believe anything at all about repentance, then we would be remiss not to know when we ourselves have been misled and need to change and be changed. If I might be a bit frank here, this really is not rocket science. If we are going to have a ministry that is at all fruitful, we will need to be deeply involved in a transformative way of life ourselves. And if we have taught others to not allow fear to have the last word in their life, then neither should we. Whatever fear we might have of what it means to give up our cherished beliefs and our ways of thinking about trying harder, that is not a good enough reason to push this aside and squash the work which God Himself wants to do in us. None of us meant to harm the way of truth, but we were all mistaken about how to live this life in the Kingdom. So let it stop with us. Let us begin in all humility to admit we did not know what God was doing, but we want to learn.

Know, too, that we do not have to make this journey alone. Many thoughtful Christians have been on this path for a long time. I am sure there have been remnants all through history. But sometime around 1985 God began a restorative work, the likes of which we have not seen since the Great Awakenings.[17] Since then, leaders and laypersons by the thousands

---

17 In my opinion, Richard Foster's *Celebration of Discipline* (1978) and Dallas Willard's *The Spirit of the Disciplines* (1988) marked a turning point in modern Christian thought. A few other authors around that time also wrote similar themes (e.g. M Robert Mulholland Jr).

have begun to rediscover this approach to Kingdom life. But it is still only a minority of the Church, and there is much to do in order to restore the Body as a whole to its rightful place. My hope is that we will live to see this wonderful movement flourish in our time.

Whatever else this means, we must begin to look at our mission and ministry though a new set of lenses. For it is not only our task to bring the gospel to our lost and dying world, but we are now also faced with the task of bringing the good news back to the Church itself. We need to help our people recover their true inheritance, and become new creations from the inside out. To that end, I would offer a few more thoughts.

**Jump-Starting Transformation**

One of the most important observations about this whole process is the fact that God has given us multiple points of intervention, any one of which can jump-start our growth and restoration. To be specific, every element of this model interacts with and enhances every other facet, such that an increase or improvement in one area will foster growth in other areas as well.

That means when we build a stronger community, we are then more able to mature in our relational abilities, which in turn will foster how we engage with God. Or if we encounter a corrective experience that renews our faith in God, then we will be more willing to surrender to whatever else He wants to do in us, and thus discover more about what it means to participate in our own formation. Or if we commit ourselves to being more intentional, that may be the means by which we encounter truth in ways that radically changes how we see who we are and whose we are.

To put it another way, a breakthrough in any one part of the model will not only move us along in our personal transformation, but it will also foster *the process* of transformation itself, making future breakthroughs and changes even more accessible. And the great news is that this can begin for any one of us anywhere in the model!

We need to truly grasp this, because we are all in different places in our journey and in need of different experiences and resources in order to renew our pursuit of God. One person might need to experience real love, while another might need to surrender their self-effort, and yet a third person might need to shed their anti-transformational theology. No one solution will jump-start this work for everyone.

That is also why one person will come away from a conference totally on fire for God, while another person will say it was boring. Or one person will find a Celebrate Recovery group that gives them a new lease on life, while their friend will say, "it doesn't do anything for me." It is all true. Because we all need different things in order to move on to the next step of our transformation into the people God created us to be.

But of course the flip side to all this is the fact that no one ministry can be the ultimate solution to everyone's path to life as God intended. And that brings us to our next observation about this process of change.

### Dropping the N-I-H Syndrome

During the 1970's and 80's the software industry I worked in was very different from the present environment. Everything was new in those days, and we guarded our in-house developments with a vigilance that would be hard to match anywhere. We had little use for what other companies were creating at the time, and would rather write a needed product ourselves than buy it from someone else. We called it the "Not-Invented-Here" syndrome. If it was not invented here, we do not need it or want it.

Unfortunately, we sometimes see the NIH syndrome at work in our Christian organizations. Churches will often insist on developing their own curriculum while ignoring the good work which others have contributed to the Body of Christ. Para-church ministries often spring up around issues that churches may fail to address – which is a good thing in itself. But sometimes their zeal and focus overtake their vision and they begin to feel as if anyone who is not part of their organization is missing the real deal or is not as concerned about important matters as they are. And if their work visibly benefits other people and churches, they may even be tempted to believe they are the be-all and end-all of God's mission for the Church.

The truth is that transformation is far too great and varied for any one ministry or organization to encompass all that it entails. If anything, the bird's eye view of transformation outlined in this book ought to make it very clear that transformation is a multifaceted process that orchestrates far more elements than any one person or any one group can fully incorporate into their ministry. Any claim to have isolated the entire process to a simple formula is missing just how comprehensive this is, and their approach will necessarily be too reductionistic to foster life-long spiritual growth.

Individually, we are far too small to grasp all that God has for us. To acknowledge our limitations only makes sense. And that leads us to the next observation, which is the flip side of ending the NIH syndrome.

### Balancing Our Critiques and Approvals

Not only do individuals need other people in their life in order to become who God intends for them to be, ministries need each other as well. One organization may have developed a life-giving ministry to the homeless, in which the givers are blessed as much as the receivers. Another organization may be the birthplace of a life-giving recovery group where people can heal from their past. Still another might know more about spiritual formation and how to engage with God.

Since we cannot possibly be proficient in all things, it only makes sense for us to network with other ministries to discover what each of us brings to the Body of Christ. Other people and organizations have studied and practiced certain areas in depth – areas in which we may have had little if any training – and consequently have been able to make wonderful advances in important matters of Kingdom life that are new to us. As we are willing to learn from the work of others, we benefit both personally and organizationally. None of us will live long enough to reinvent the wheel in every area of transformation. Ministries need each another in order to gain even a cursory introduction to the many facets of growth and change.

Among other things, this implies that we ought to validate other ministries for what they offer, and not dismiss them out of hand because of the areas in which they are lacking. Bear in mind that I am referring here to ministries that contribute in some significant way to the transformation of those they are called to serve. If people are being changed for the better by those ministries, then we would do well to understand that the resources in that place are meeting a real need for those who are at a particular place in their journey. On that basis we can affirm what good they are doing, even if we differ from them in other ways that are important to us. If we had to have everything right in order to be validated by others, there are precious few of us who would qualify.[18]

At the same time it is important to notice what resources are lacking or unavailable from a particular ministry. Sometimes this is obvious, such as when an emergency food shelf provides fairly limited spiritual help, whereas a prayer ministry may not provide food. These ministries could make excellent use of each others' resources and affirm each other for the good they offer, while at the same time be fully aware of what the other ministry does not provide – and do so without any contempt or condemnation. Of course most ministry comparisons are more nuanced than that, such as when one organization offers incredible Christian educational materials but has little understanding of spiritual formation. We can affirm the good education they provide and the work they have done in order to offer that education, while at the same time be aware of what areas their ministry does not address. This is all good and normal because no one ministry can do everything needed in the Kingdom.

18 "Whoever is not against us is for us" (Mk.9:40).

Accepting the natural limitations of our ministries ought to actually encourage us to refer people to other ministries when we are unable to help them where they are in their journey. We cannot be all things to all people, and we do them a disservice when we insist that they restrict themselves to whatever it is we have to offer. If their next step requires assistance that our ministry cannot provide well, then we should point them toward another place that can help them better.

But in addition to validating what is good and being aware of what is not offered, it is also important to discern any area in which a ministry is blatantly anti-transformational or teaching things that are anti-identity or anti-relational in nature. Far too many Christian organizations still teach legalism as if it were the core of discipleship. Some even oppose important matters of how to participate well in transformation, because they have misunderstood those means and have labeled them as New Age or otherwise "unbiblical." Still others are simply repeating what they have been taught, totally unaware of the implications of what they are teaching and how it actually undermines the process of transformation.

Whatever the reason for anti-transformational teaching, it needs to be unmasked for what it is and exposed for its destructive potential. The damage it does to the larger Body is incalculable and needs to stop. Even so, we need to be careful with our critique and begin in love and hope that those whom we are confronting will be willing and able to see the truth and change how they present the Kingdom to others. Only when they have demonstrated an unwillingness to change do we have any reason to oppose them more vocally or more publicly, and even then we need to discern how and when, and whether it is necessary.[19]

Learning to work together with the greater Body of Christ and doing our utmost to accomplish that should be our primary orientation toward

---

19 One significant example is Charles Ryrie's adamant defense of his seriously truncated version of the gospel, which has great potential to do harm.

other ministries. This is an important part of doing ministry at all. And when we see how comprehensive God's plan for transformation truly is, we can be sure that we need other parts of the Body more than we know.

## Identifying Ministries that Foster Transformation

This book would be incomplete if it did not include at least few examples of ministries and authors who are making significant contributions to the larger community of believers in offering substantial resources in this area of personal transformation. While I cannot provide a comprehensive list of all effective resources and ministries, I will identify a few that I am aware of which are doing a great job in one or more of the areas highlighted in this model.

Some of these ministries focus more on the specific causes of transformation, others work primarily with helping people participate well, and still others work with creating a robust context to foster transformation. My goal in providing these examples is to help the reader know what is looks like when a ministry truly grasps the means which are available to us for change. While I am certain there are dozens of ministries which could be included here, my hope is that the ones identified will be sufficient for the intended purpose.

### Transformation Prayer Ministry (TPM)

Originally known as Theophostic[20] Prayer Ministry and developed by Ed Smith, TPM is an approach to inner healing that focuses on the power of truth when it is revealed directly to us by God. Many thousands of people have had amazing encounters with God through this form of prayer

20 From the Greek *theos* (God) and *photos* (light), Theophostic was founded on the premise that God's light can reveal truth that transforms our mind.

ministry, often resulting in significant change in areas of their life which had been problematic for years.

The basic premise of this approach to inner healing is that many of our emotional and spiritual problems result directly from things we have come to believe about ourselves and about the things we have experienced. These internal beliefs are quite often terribly flawed, and Ed refers to these as the "lies" which keep us in bondage. Such lies can be deeply entrenched in our mind and highly resistant to change, no matter how unreasonable or unrealistic they may be. But when God reveals the truth about those lies and the truth about how He sees us and our experiences, our mind can let go of these implicit lies and embrace the truth. And since much of how we live is determined by what we assume to be true, this type of healing can have a phenomenal impact on the rest of our life.

It is worth noting that from time to time, Ed has been criticized for not widening his ministry to include other factors relating to spiritual healing and growth. But such a critique may be somewhat short-sighted. What we need to understand is that his dedication to this one particular principle has benefited the Kingdom tremendously.

Perhaps a comparison to other disciplines will help to shed some light on this. We all know that major advances in science have often come from a researcher focusing on a single bacteria for several decades until an answer finally emerges that eradicates a disease. And if it were not for their intense research in such a small area, they would have never had their breakthrough. The same can be said for Ed's research on the nature of truth and its ability to change lives. The reason this ministry has impacted so many people and continues to do so is because one man dedicated his life to understanding one of the ways in which God transforms lives.

In terms of our model, Ed has made incredible contributions to our understanding and practice of transformation by truth.

## The Immanuel Approach

Another researcher whose work has impacted many people is Karl Lehman. As a psychiatrist and Christian counselor, he spent thousands of hours pouring over his notes trying to make sense of why some people were able to encounter God for inner healing fairly easily while others were unable to do so. What emerged from his patience and effort is what is now known around the world as The Immanuel Approach.

What Karl noticed was that in our efforts to receive healing for old wounds and other life issues, ministers and prayer-recipients alike often tend to over-focus on the problems the person has faced, to the extent that the person receiving ministry becomes overwhelmed with their pain and loses their connection with God for the healing He can offer them. By shifting the focus of the ministry session away from looking at the problem and instead paying attention to how we can stay connected with God and how to deal with the barriers that get in the way of our connection, Karl discovered that healing often came more quickly and the process was far less painful for the person.

Karl's emphasis on working with God to remove all barriers between God and us is an invaluable contribution in and of itself. Furthermore, his research in regard to applying this focus to the area of emotional and psychological healing has greatly advanced our understanding of how we can stay connected with God in emotionally difficult times. What is more, it turns out that his approach to inner healing requires very little initial training in order to pass it on, making it one of the most transferable tools we have as Christians.[21]

In terms of our model, this ministry takes great care in helping people maintain an interactive connection with God even when it is difficult to do

---

21 Yet despite its fundamental simplicity, this approach to inner healing has tremendous implications, which Karl has researched in depth. See the full analysis in his book, *The Immanuel Approach*.

so, and to engage with God for healing, especially when in need of either God's truth or love as a means of transformation.

**HeartSync Ministries**

Another ministry that has been quietly growing for the last twenty years or so was founded by an Anglican minister by the name of Father Andrew Miller. Over a period of many years, Father Andrew has helped several thousand people from all walks of life recover from very difficult issues, and in the process he has developed an approach to inner healing that goes far deeper, encompasses more aspects of our humanity, and produces greater change than one might ever think possible. Of course, due to its extensive nature, we cannot do it justice here in a few paragraphs. What follows then is a mere glimpse of what this work entails.

At the core of HeartSync ministry is the recognition that human beings are fairly complex creatures with multiple ways of dealing with trauma and pain, all of which can significantly reshape our inner world, with very few conscious decisions involved in the process. Along these lines, one of our most common responses to emotional or psychological pain is to compartmentalize our mind and soul, effectively limiting our day-to-day awareness of past traumas with their related overwhelming emotions, so that we can continue to function as well as possible in our daily life.

These inner divisions happen more or less automatically, and are initially often quite effective in helping us cope. But God never meant for us to live with a divided heart, and over time these divisions almost always become self-defeating. HeartSync's approach to inner healing takes this inner dividedness very seriously, slowing the process down to where every aspect of our heart can engage with God for the healing we need.

One of the great contributions of this ministry is the way in which it helps us to go deeper and engage more facets of our inner life in a single healing session. In terms of our model of transformation, HeartSync focuses very deliberately on enlisting our intentionality and deepening our receptivity to what God wants to do. Ministry sessions also often involve corrective experiences with God from multiple angles, as well as profound experiences of God's love and care, accompanied by deep cleansing of pain and trauma. With all these elements of transformation present in a single prayer time, the results of this approach to healing are truly amazing.

### Life Model Works (LMW)

Formerly known as Shepherd's House of Pasadena, California, this organization's best contribution has been a wonderfully ideal model of how God designed us to grow up and thrive as human beings. Beginning with the premise that God is relational and He created us to be relational beings, and drawing from thousands of hours of clinical practice as a knowledge base about why people thrive and why they fail to thrive, LMW laid out a map of how God intended for us to grow up emotionally and relationally, and what resources are needed to get us from infancy to full maturity. A major part of this process also involved better understanding of Christian community and what is required in order for such a group to provide a context in which people can become all that God intended.

Among other things, they have developed a detailed model of what it takes to move from infancy to child level, adult level, parent level, and even elder level maturity. Usually referred to as the *Life Model,* this ideal description of human development describes the most important emotional and relational steps required in order to move from one stage of maturity to the next, and highlights the key attributes of each level.

Given that human development and spiritual development are highly interdependent, the Life Model provides essential detail for building a stronger context for transformation. This includes both our need for a life-giving community and our need for a relationally-based approach to human maturity. While there are many other authors and organizations who have contributed to these contextual areas, very few have attempted the sort of comprehensive description that comes from Life Model Works.

### Other Spiritual Formation Resources

Again, many good authors have contributed greatly to the area of how to participate well in our own journey of transformation. For example, I can heartily recommend most any of the books by people like David Benner, Ruth Haley Barton, James Bryan Smith, Jan Johnson, M. Robert Mulholland Jr, and John Ortberg, to name a few. Of course the work of Dallas Willard goes without saying. In addition there are many para-church ministries that are doing amazing work with helping Christians everywhere become more like Jesus, such as, Alive and Well (alivewell.org), and Healing Center International (godhealstoday.org).

Drawing from the groundwork laid down by many of these authors, the book *Forming: A Work of Grace*, and its related course *Forming: Change by Grace* both offer a foundation of theology and the practical means by which we can engage with God in ways that change us from the inside out. In terms of our model, the *Forming* course is a highly practical introduction to the various elements of *participation*, along with critical elements of formationally sound theology that provide an important context for this whole process.

In particular, these authors and organizations are helping Christians move away from the performance-driven religion most of us learned, and instead develop a relationally based approach to growth and transformation.

## Final Thoughts

If I may repeat a few words from the Preface, when I stand back and look at this journey toward a life characterized by ongoing transformation I am struck by a most peculiar realization – that transformation does not emerge from any spectacular event or angelic vision or any other special experience available only to the super-spiritual. *Rather, it is due to hundreds, if not thousands of tiny steps available to almost anyone, regardless of where they begin.* The abundant life is not a far-away dream available only to people like Hudson Taylor or John Wesley. The wonders which God mapped out for us in the New Testament are accessible to the very least among us. The great mystery is not how to find this path that leads to life. What is truly perplexing is why it is not more commonplace among professing Christians.

God did not invade human history and offer Himself as a sacrifice just to make it possible for us to go to heaven in our next life. He wants us to know Him and live with Him now as children of the King! That means being changed from what we were into people who are taking on the very image of Christ, offering goodness and love to those around us.

I am fairly certain this model I am offering is still incomplete in some ways. It is but a modest proposal for helping the Christian world move away from its programs of self-effort and religious activity, toward a vision of faith that actually changes lives as a matter of course. Transformation need not be rare, nor unpredictable. We can learn how to foster and expect this kind of change so that we become more and more the persons God created us to be.

More than anything, my hope is that the Christian world will reignite its passion for learning how to follow Jesus and how to be changed by engaging with Him. Transformation is easily within reach and highly accessible for all who will pursue God for the life we always knew should be possible!

# Acknowledgments

Due to the very nature of spiritual formation and the fact that this model is an eclectic compilation drawn from dozens of sources over the years, it would be impossible for me to recall everyone who has fostered my belief in transformation or helped to shape my understanding of how it happens. But a few people do come to mind as having been particularly influential, and it seems important to identify them here, because nothing in this book is uniquely mine apart from connecting the dots in a way I have not seen before. Almost all of the particulars are things I learned from others.

More than anyone else, Dallas Willard has altered my worldview of what it means to be a Christian. When I began reading *The Divine Conspiracy* in late 1998, it was truly water to my soul. It was the book I had been looking for my entire adult life. After that I could not get enough of what he wrote, and I attended every event I could where he was speaking. This present book is in fact meant to be a complementary work to *The Renovation of the Heart*, an incredibly important work in which Dallas lays out not only the basics of transformation, but a detailed map of what it is within us that needs to be transformed. He was truly one of the greatest minds of the twentieth century, with a heart to match. And much of the Christian world has yet to recognize the significance of his many contributions.

I would also like to acknowledge the impact of those who have spent many years unraveling the mysteries of inner healing, in particular Ed Smith of Transformation Prayer Ministry, Karl Lehman's development of the Immanual Approach, and Father Andrew Miller who pioneered HeartSync Ministry. Their dedication and experience have been invaluable to me in my own journey, as well as highly influential in shaping my understanding of the Goodness of God and how much He wants to restore us.

There are many authors as well, perhaps too many to name. But a few who have impacted me most are Mark Virkler (*Communion with God*), David Benner (many titles), Jan Johnson (*When the Soul Listens*), and James Bryan Smith (*The Good and Beautiful God*).

I would be remiss if I did not also mention the ministry of Life Model Works and their contributions over the years to my understanding of how God designed us to live in community and to grow up relationally and emotionally as well as spiritually. Without their emphasis, I might well have overlooked the need for a robust relational context for transformation.

In terms of my personal journey, no one has impacted me more than my wife Jan. She has brought more love, truth, and corrective experience into my life than is possible to recount. Together we have made a life of pursuing God for all the good He has for us (though often haltingly), including learning how to flesh that out between the two of us and how to offer it to others as well. Jan's amazing gift for helping other wounded travelers connect with the Lord for healing and recovery has not only been a wonder to witness, but has changed my life in more ways than I can say.

Finally, none of this would have been possible if it were not for the mercy and grace of God who has seen fit to rescue me from my despair and self-rejection, and to give me a hope and life that I could not have imagined thirty years ago. He is my constant Companion, my Healer, my Mentor, and my God. And for some reason He gave me a heart and mind that enjoys sifting through mounds of data in order to try and make sense of His great goodness in this very strange world. Then He pours in resources and keeps me from straying too far off course.

That is why these books come to be at all.

# Bibliography – for Additional Reading

**Regarding Truth**

David Takle, *The Truth About Lies and Lies About Truth*

Ed Smith, *Healing Life's Hurts*

**Regarding Love**

David Benner, *Surrender to Love*

Brennan Manning, *Abba's Child*

**Regarding Participation**

David Takle, *Forming: A Work of Grace*

David Takle, *Forming: Change by Grace* (experiential course)

David Takle, *Whispers of My Abba*

Jan Johnson, *When the Soul Listens*

**Regarding Community and Human Maturity**

James Friesen, et al, *The Life Model*

E James Wilder, *The Complete Guide to Living With Men*

**Regarding Spiritual Formation and Transformation**

Dallas Willard, *The Spirit of the Disciplines*

Dallas Willard, *The Renovation of the Heart*

M. Robert Mulholland, Jr. *Shaped by the Word*

**Regarding a Formational Context**

Dallas Willard, *The Divine Conspiracy*

James Bryan Smith, *The Good and Beautiful God*

Curt Thompson, *Anatomy of the Soul*

**Regarding Inner Healing**

Karl Lehman, *Outsmarting Yourself*

Karl Lehman, *The Immanuel Approach*

**Online Resources and Ministries**

KingdomFormation.org – my personal site

HeartSyncMinistries.org – Father Andrew Miller

GodHealsToday.org – Healing Center International

AliveWell.org – Alive and Well (Immanuel training)

LifeModelWorks.org – Life Model Works

SpiritualLeadership.com – The Leadership Institute

ImmanuelApproach.com – Karl Lehman's Ministry

TransformationPrayer.org – Ed Smith

JanJohnson.org – Jan Johnson

DWillard.org – Dallas Willard's work

Renovare.org – Renovare Organization (Richard Foster)

Please note that there are dozens of other resources which could be included here. But rather than overwhelm the reader with options, my goal was to highlight those which have been most significant in my own journey and which I believe will be helpful to others.

If you enjoyed *Transformation by Design*,
you will love
***The Truth About Lies and Lies About Truth***

How God transforms our mind by Truth!

Available from Amazon or
KingdomFormation.org
(also in Kindle format)

Made in the USA
Las Vegas, NV
05 January 2023